A Tennessee Landscape
People
and Places

Prescott Howard Elizabeth

A Tennessee Landscape
People
and Places

1996 Tennessee Writers Alliance Anthology

FIRST EDITION.

Cool Springs Press™, Tennessee Writers Alliance anthology logotype™, and cover
design property of Cool Springs Press, Publishers.

Cover design by Hound Dog Studio, Nashville, TN
Cover photo © by Chris Miner
Book design by Nat Akin
Set in Cochin

Library of Congress Cataloging-in-Publication Data

A Tennessee Landscape, People, and Places: Tennessee Writers Alliance 1996
Anthology / Nat Akin, general editor. — 1st ed.
ISBN 1-888608-32-3 (pbk.)
1. American literature—Tennessee. 2. American literature—20th century.

Contents

Acknowledgements

The Tennessee Writers Alliance, Inc. gives grateful acknowledgements to the:

Women's National Book Association for its encouragement, nurturing, and unwavering support;

Tennessee Arts Commission for its financial support and guidance; Tennessee Humanities Council for its support of the goals and objectives and ongoing efforts of TWA;

Advisory Board and Board of Directors, volunteers past and present for their vision, talents, and consistent hard work to keep the organization viable;

many corporate businesses, organizations, universities, and individuals who have supported TWA in invaluable and unsung ways;

editorial committee members who burned the midnight oil to bring the first editorial printing of this anthology to fruition: Ronna Blaser, Bryan Curtis, Jill Carpenter, Connie Green, John Reaves, Bobby Rogers, Amy Lyles Wilson, and Tommie Morton Young; and TWA Executive Director Blandy Costello for assistance from start to finish of this project;

manuscript selection committee members who volunteered their talents and time in the selection of prose and poetry on the following pages: Chet Flippo, David Hunter, and Jack Reese;

publisher Roger Waynick, editor Nat Akin, marketing director Hank McBride, and the staff of Cool Springs Press for their faith in the worthiness of this project;

and most of all, grateful acknowledgments and thanks to the writers who have contributed to this debut anthology.

Emma J. Wisdom, Chair, TWA Anthology Committee
October 1996

A History of the Tennessee Writers Alliance
As I Remember
Phyllis Gobbell, President, 1994-1996

In this year that marks Tennessee's bicentennial, the Tennessee Writers Alliance is also celebrating a birthday. We are five years old, and consistent with the reminiscent mood in the state, we are also looking back to our beginnings and recalling the milestones in our short history.

The idea of a statewide organization for writers had long been deliberated by literary groups and individual writers in Tennessee, but the real groundwork was laid by the Nashville Chapter of the Women's National Book Association (WNBA). Looking to the North Carolina Writers' Network for inspiration, WNBA formed a committee in 1990 to investigate the need for a writers network in Tennessee.

The WNBA writers network committee sought the advice and support of the Tennessee Arts Commission (TAC). A meeting with the TAC Literary Panel in the spring of 1990 resulted in plans to conduct a survey among writers in the state to determine their critical needs and to invite Marsha Warren, Executive Director of the North Carolina Writers' Network, to address interested writers at the Southern Festival of Books on the benefits of a statewide writers network. The TAC gave its encouragement to these plans in the form of a $500 technical grant.

During the summer, a needs assessment questionnaire was sent to 360 writers across Tennessee. Out of this number, 210 respondents overwhelmingly endorsed the idea of some type of statewide organization that would benefit writers. At the Southern Festival of Books, Marsha Warren spoke to an enthusiastic audience of approximately 125 and inspired us with North Carolina's great success story. A steering committee was formed, and plans began in earnest to address the structure, activities, and services of the organization with the working name, Tennessee Writers Network.

One of the first challenges of the steering committee was to find an immediate source of funding during the organizational process. A statewide appeal to approximately 600 writers resulted in $2100 in founder contributions, and we became the Tennessee Writers Alliance with 107 charter members. The Tennessee Writers Alliance, Inc. was officially incorporated on February 21, 1991.

During the winter and spring of 1991, the steering committee selected a board of directors, board of advisors, and officers of the corporation, formalized our relationship with our sponsoring organization WNBA, and adopted bylaws for the corporation. While it is impossible to name the many individuals who worked tirelessly during this critical period, the attorney-writer who spearheaded our effort and led us through the legal maze of incorporation cannot go unmentioned. Lee Wilson donated her legal services, which included drafting bylaws, filing our charter with the state, and setting in motion our application for non-profit status with the federal government.

The first meeting of the board of directors was June 21, 1991. Several committees were formed to oversee the activities of the Alliance, and we moved forward with ambitious plans for the months ahead. Our first newsletter was published and a membership brochure printed. We hired our first part-time executive director. We applied for and received a grant from the Tennessee Arts Commission. The Alliance sponsored a panel of literary agents and packagers at the Southern Festival of Books. By mid-October we looked back over our initial accomplishments and took a deep breath. The Alliance was solid.

Our membership in January 1992 numbered 240. By May 1992, we had 331 members. It has been an ongoing process to redefine and expand our services. The Alliance has sponsored an event each year at the Southern Festival of Books. Publication of our newsletter has increased from four to six times a year. We sponsored our first literary contest in 1993 and received 260 short fiction entries. The next year we received 643 entries in poetry. The competition has become an annual event, alternating fiction and poetry. Winners are awarded at a ceremony at the Southern Festival of Books. Finalists read their work during the year on occasions we call "An Evening with the Alliance." Initially, we sponsored three workshops in East,

West, and Middle Tennessee annually. In the 1996-97 fiscal year, we will sponsor twelve workshops across the state.

Through these five years, we have been fortunate to find excellent leadership for the Alliance. Board members volunteer service with a spirit of dedication and generosity. The financial compensation for part-time executive director does not in any way reflect the many hours that the individuals who have held this position have given to the cause. We have been ably served by Susan Knowles, Donna Tauscher, Amy Lynch, Michael Gillespie, and presently by Blandy Costello. Each in a distinctive way has made a lasting contribution to the organization.

To the Women's National Book Association, Nashville Chapter, and the Tennessee Arts Commission we owe a great debt of gratitude for nurturing, encouraging, and supporting us. To all the corporate and individual sponsors who have made possible the continuing expansion of services and projects, we offer our sincere appreciation.

Our most exciting new project has been the publication of this anthology. *A Tennessee Landscape, People, and Places* is the first issue in what we hope will be another annual tradition for the Tennessee Writers Alliance. We can think of no better way to celebrate our birthday than to provide a showcase for the creative works of our members. We hope the selections capture the unique spirit of Tennessee writers.

A Tennessee Landscape, People, and Places
Preface

As I write this, Tennessee has come of age. It's our 200th year and we're ready for anything and everything—eager to take on the challenges of a new millennium, anxious to be a part of the cyberspace age. Yet, even in this day of E-mail and computerized checking accounts and phones on planes, we still derive great pleasure from reading the written word. In most homes, one or two newspapers arrive daily and numerous magazines fill our mailboxes, not to mention newsletters, flyers, letters, bills, etc. So how do any of us find time to read a good book, let alone write one? Why do we even want to? That's a question the Tennessee Writers Alliance agonized over as we planned for this publication; a question that was not easily answered.

Publishing this anthology is the completion of a long-time goal for the Alliance—a goal to showcase our best members and to let the whole world know how talented and diverse Tennessee writers can be. That's why you'll find the famous and the not-famous-yet writer here. Not every writer made it (there were guidelines that had to be met), but for those of you who did, being published in a statewide anthology means you are now a part of Tennessee's writing legacy.

As the state's premiere writing organization, the Alliance has a mission to encourage writers and to take part in the writing-related issues and concerns within Tennessee.

Still, we worried about how to best fulfill our mission and put together a volume of writing that would be both lasting and meaningful.

As I look at my own collection of anthologies, it becomes more clear that an anthology can be timeless, like the Bible, or, it can be a showcase, a collection of the best, as in a collection of award winners. Its theme can celebrate a single idea or issue (*Some Say Tomato* [Mariflo Stephens 1993]) or the life of someone well known (*A House of Gathering—Poets on May Sarton's Poetry* [University of Tennessee Press, 1993]). Let's face it,

13

sometimes publishing an anthology is a way to raise much-needed funds.

One of my most recent anthology purchases—*Downhome*, Harcourt Brace, 1995—"sold" me with only the cover as I read the long list of Southern women writers. I smile remembering personal encounters I've had with some of these talented ladies—some I know intimately by tone and talent etched in a way only that particular artist can paint. Just thinking of them, I recall a favorite line of verse or a book that was so good I sat up all night to finish it.

Still another collection reminds me of my roots and the East Tennessee Valley where I was born and still call home. *Voices from the Valley, Selections from the Knoxville Writers' Guild, 1994*, is also full of familiar names, many of them autographed across the top of their story or poem.

Many of the same names will be found in this Alliance volume that have been published in other anthologies, like *Home Works*, a long-awaited collection that the Tennessee Arts Commission has just published, or some of the ones I've previously mentioned. Each book has its own flavor. Like the grape picked from the same vine, it can produce a flavorful chardonnay or a robust burgundy. *A Tennessee Landscape, People, and Places* is a pen and ink harvest—our best crop compilation.

Too, there's a certain mystery about picking up a single book by several authors. As you scan through the names hoping to find one you recognize, a title or a word reaches out and you find yourself reading a poem or a story, and suddenly you've found a new friend.

Maybe that's WHY. Whether an anthology represents the founding of friendships or the passage of time, it's not just a reflection of who we are but all that we have been and, maybe most importantly, all that we can be!

Patricia A. Hope
Chairman of the Board, 1996

Connie Abston

At The Civil Rights Museum

Somehow I do not think I will forget
The family of three who preceded me.
There was something, maybe the way the father's hand
Rested gently on his son's neck, that made me want to follow.
In the main room, the walls flickered with films
Of atrocity—people beaten back with fire hoses,
Arrests, taunting shouts, the dreaded KKK,
With blaring audio making it vividly real.
I was the only white that day, and so
Ashamed for the sins of my people that I held back
And let the others go their way.
It was the mother who turned, lifting her arm
As if to take me in—I have kept that moment
For it was then, you see, I understood the dream.

CONNIE ABSTON is a fifty-something mother of eight (four her own and four inherited). She is a Memphis native who has become a "later life" writer of poetry and short fiction.

Margrethe Ahlschwede
Balloon Walker

My father has appeared. And I am mightily reassured, believe me. When Ward and I, just after our forty-ninth birthdays, decided to move away from everybody who ever meant anything to us and settle in Tennessee, I wondered most about my father, how he would find me, how I would find him. but he's come from the beyond again and, as I say, I'm mightily reassured.

Everything Ward and I know about growing up, about raising children, about living our lives, we learned in Missouri. How could we move from such a nest? How could we leave all the good people who helped nurse Scotty through appendicitis, Annie through pneumonia, Ward through gall bladder surgery, and me through untold hours of talk about my upbringing. We had spent nearly our entire adult lives in Missouri. What did we know about Tennessee? What did my father? He had spent six hours in the state the year he and my mother drove from their home in Nebraska to North Carolina to visit us when Ward was in graduate school. They had come through Nashville, Knoxville, and Gatlinburg, on through the Appalachians to Asheville, then north up the Blue Ridge Parkway to Deep Gap and then off on 421 to North Wilkesboro, and south and across to Raleigh. I still remember seeing my father jump out of the car at the duplex, the way I rushed down the steps to give him a kiss hello, his comment as he described the incredible scenery on their trip: "And people in Nebraska try to promote tourism."

By then Ward and I had been in North Carolina nearly two years. Our first year there, spring unveiling itself to us, I had written to my parents about the camellias on the bush right

18

outside our back door—heady, rich, creamy white blooms, enough to pick. In Nebraska camellias grew in florist shops and young men bought them as singles with a bow and a pin, slipped in crisp plastic for the Y-Teen Snow Ball in December or the senior prom in May. Camellias on bushes were unbelievable to me. And everybody had them. And nearly everybody had fig bushes—actual bushes with figs. Nothing prepared me for that first spring in North Carolina.

That second year when my parents visited, the azaleas were even more lush—deep pink and white bouquets spilling in profusion over the low brick retaining walls on the campus, dogwoods a blizzard of white and pink on Dixie Trail, the street perpendicular to the end of our block. I had put a bowl of camellias on the table. And then when my parents drove off a week after their arrival they took with them a magnolia bloom my mother had torn from a tree on the campus. As my father backed out of the drive I could see my mother holding the flower by the stem, leaning forward into the nest of the bloom and I imagined her lungs filling with the heavy lemon scent as I waved them good-by.

Beginning after my father's death seven years later—by then Ward had gotten his degree and we were back in the midwest, not Nebraska, but close—Columbia, Missouri, and Scotty and Annie in pre-school—I saw my father at least once a year on Pentecost when the young people at the Methodist church were confirmed. The pastor always got a weather balloon, blew it up, and hung it from one of the beams. But before he and the janitor hoisted it up, he cut out flame shapes from red construction paper and printed on each flame with a thick black marker the name of one of the young people who had completed confirmation that year. He then taped the flames on the balloon. It was such a magical sight the first year—a light blue-green iridescent globe slowly circling over the pulpit, easing in its rotation from the center aisle to the side, as if the moon mysteriously had moved out of the heavens and come personally to us, big enough and close enough that we actually might

19

touch it, or cause it to turn if we poofed a shot of breath sound-ly enough in the right direction. Each year I looked forward to seeing that balloon, to discovering the given names of our baby-sitters and the other young people we knew from church. They were Marti, Kris, Nate, Skip. But on Pentecost they became such beautiful, long, full names — Michaela Marianne, Alexandra Kristine, Nathaniel Benjamin, Jordan Wesley. To my mind, discovering these real names each year was as much a revelation as Pentecost itself.

It was with that first Pentecost in Missouri that I saw my father from death. In the balloon. Annie had tucked herself into my lap and Scotty sat beside me, his knees bent, the soles of his Buster Browns slapping the wooden seat of the pew. Their heads were turned up, their tiny noses pointed in the air, their blond curls fallen back as they watched the balloon magi-cally glide and turn away, glide and turn back. As they watched, I read the flames pronouncing each name as the flame bearing it rolled near us, swaying and turning on the balloon — Alexandra Kristine, Nathaniel Benjamin, Martin. Martin.

My father, Martin. I gasped as I said Martin into Annie's ear and then I caught myself. The balloon rotated fur-ther and slowly I began to see that the name hadn't been Martin at all. I had been Michaela Marianne. But for a moment, in that short space of time it took me to say Martin, it was as if my father actually had been there, hanging in the air above us, coming that close, being that present to me, to Ward, and to our children.

On the ride home from church, I asked Ward about weather balloons, how they worked. They're tethered, he said, just like the one in the sanctuary. I couldn't imagine how high, how long a tether. If it were tethered, Ward said, there would be direct electrical contact between ground and the balloon with its backpack of instruments. What would the instruments measure? Oh, minimum and maximum temperatures, wind velocity, that kind of thing, Ward said.

I imagined my father in his soft-soled slippers up inside

the balloon, unbuckling the little backpack, taking the instruments out and settling them onto the bottom curve of the balloon, making sure they measured what they were supposed to measure. Or if it isn't tethered, Ward said, the balloon could be connected to the ground through radio telemetry.

And I imagined all the young confirmands—our babysitters—trying to make radio contact with God, each one holding a receiver, all of them standing in a row at the airport trying to get in touch. Hello? God? It's me, a confirmand. And my father, balancing delicately to the inside curve of the balloon clicking the instruments together, sending a crackle of a signal down, enough to convince the young people that yes, there is a God.

From then on, Pentecost became as important to me as Christmas and Easter. Every year, sitting on the wooden pew in the sanctuary, watching the iridescent pentecost moon circling above the altar, I read off to myself the new grand names that filled the flames. And each Pentecost as the weather balloon rotated, the flames moving above and before the congregation, I said the name Martin. Those mornings I believed my father was as present in those red construction paper flames and as present with me as were the children who came forward to promise themselves to God.

And now, no iridescent moon and no Pentecost flames, my father has made contact. Totally unexpectedly we had moved to Jackson, Tennessee, so Ward could manage a boar test-station. Jackson wasn't all that far from Columbia so it wasn't as if we were moving to the ends of the earth. We shocked ourselves as much as we shocked our friends with our thinking, but the spirit of adventure seized us. Scotty and Annie had left home for college and graduate school and we could pretend we were retiring, even though Ward still would be working.

We had moved in the spring. A substitute finished out the year for me at Springdale Elementary where I had taught first grade all the years we lived in Columbia. Our move south matched the bursting of Tennessee blooms—iris in every front yard, buttercups along every country road, dogwoods in white, pink, and rose. We marveled at the spring—gayer and brighter than any of our springs in Columbia.

And the clatter and chitter of the birds. Birds we never knew existed. Birds we'd only seen in other people's bird books now were in our trees, darting across the yard, pecking and scratching at the feeders Ward had hung in the courtyard. I became captivated by the birds—rufous-sided towhees, house finches, downy and red-breasted woodpeckers, wrens, doves. We bought a set of binoculars and a bird book for the dining room table, ready when we needed them.

The first fall in Tennessee we also learned about leaves. Our tiny forest, deep, rich green, became gold with leaves— gold driveways, gold yards. The leaves slid away from the trees and spiraled down to settle on the drive, onto the gutters, onto the mound of dirt Ward had delivered to fill in some low spots south of the house. Some days the trees rained leaves. Other days the wind spirited the leaves parallel to the horizon across the yard, the way wind spit snow in blizzards in Nebraska. Every morning when I opened the front door to pick up the *Commercial Appeal* from the porch, gold leaves carpeted the drive. When I stepped out on the sidewalk past the porch roof I could see leaves there, too, stacked inches high past the lip of the gutter. Ward bought a leaf blower and every day blew more gold leaves out of the gutters and off the drive and deck. One Saturday, listening to the drone of the blower, watching Ward guide the thick wand, I saw behind him the fall show of finches, woodpeckers, and cardinals.

"It's addictive," Ward said at dinner as we watched out the window over coffee. "It's mesmerizing to watch these birds."

"Yes," I said, thinking of my father, remembering the tiny pica print of his typewriter letters describing birds in his yard. In retrospect, I think that moment of recognition about the birds, seeing in my mind the way his letters looked as I read them, was the beginning of what led me to see my father again. That and the music.

In Columbia, I hardly ever was at home except on the weekends. And who had time for music then? But in Tennessee I didn't go back to first grade. I wanted time to rest, to think. I had unfinished quilting projects. I wanted to learn calligraphy. And I wanted to read all the Madeleine L'Engles from first to last, all the Gail Godwins, and what I was beginning to know about Tennessee writers—James Agee, Peter Taylor, Wilma Dykeman. So for the first time in my adult life I was home during the day, listening to public radio. One fall afternoon sitting on the deck, I'd left open a window. I had started a new Peter Taylor story when suddenly I thought I heard the sound of a piano—Chopin—and immediately I saw my father.

When we were growing up it was my father who tucked us into bed. Our mother taught evening school, so she made dinner for us and left my sister and me to eat with our father as she went off to teach. He was the one who helped us with homework. He was the one who tucked us in each night and said our prayers with us. He would shut out the light and say, now go to sleep girls, as he closed the door on his way into the living room and the piano. That's how my sister and I fell asleep—listening to our father playing Chopin polonaises. In bed, my eyes shut, I pictured him with his long fingers over the keys, leaning back, his arms almost stretched forward as he played the music that crept under our door.

But when I knew he had found me for sure it was on the campus at Union University. Ward and I always had tickets to arts council events in Columbia—the Boston Pops on tour, Isaac Stern the night a string broke on his violin. He had hardly missed a note moving his violin to the concertmaster's, the concertmaster handing his to Stern as if they'd practiced this exchange. So we signed up for the concert series at Union— five concerts a semester, a mix of local and national stars. Funds were short, but the arts group was doing its best.

It was the first week of November. We'd driven along

streets where mounds of gold leaves still waited for city trucks to haul them off. Nearly all the trees were bare and the night was crisp. The concert featured a tenor, a faculty member at Union. In the first part of the program he sang in German and after intermission sang Gershwin and Rogers and Hammerstein. At the conclusion of the printed program we applauded wildly. Ward and I looked at each other, impressed, applauding continually. The tenor had exited the stage, but then came back, his accompanist trailing behind him.

"I have an encore," he announced from the stage. "But I need a baritone. Is there a baritone in the house?" I thought it was a joke and mouthed to Ward, what's going on? When I looked back on the stage I saw three men—the tenor, the accompanist now seated again at the piano, and another man in tux and bow tie. The addition pulled at his lapels, faced the tenor, nodded, and turned to the audience. The tenor nodded to the accompanist. And when he began to play, that's when I knew my father had found me.

The opening notes of the piano swept to the front of the stage, up the rows of seats and settled upon me. I could have been back there, three or four or five years old, watching in our living room as my father put on the old 78 and we listened to the tenor and baritone singing the duet from *The Pearl Fisher's*. Sitting there in the concert hall at Union, I recognized it immediately. When had I heard it last? I couldn't say. But listening to these voices soar, reach, and come together, I saw my father. I was back in the room with the red walls and the white curtains, my father now reading, smoke curling up from his cigarette, his gold wire-rimmed glasses as they always sat on his nose, his head with its fringe of light blond hair. He had been in a fire when he was in his twenties and since then, had only this light crop of hair about his ears, tidy and combed. The tenor on stage had dark brown hair, a full head, and the baritone's hair was gray and wavy. Neither was as tall as my father and neither as slender. But it was him. I knew it was him. I nudged Ward on the arm and tried to say, this is it, this is the one, this is the

24

piece we always heard on the record when I was little. But it
didn't make sense and I couldn't say it straight.

After we got home from the concert I called my sister.
"You don't have to tell me. I know exactly the piece you're talking about," she said, describing the exact memory I had—the
red room, the white curtains, my father leaning over the record
player, settling the needle. The next day I found a record store
and ordered the CD, Robert Merrill and Jussi Bjorling. The
best recording ever, the clerk told me. After it finally arrived
two weeks later, I wrapped it for my sister for Christmas, and
in February, for my birthday, she sent me a tape she made from
it.

I play it now in the kitchen kneading bread. I remember
my father at dinner teasing us about how he wanted the first
heel of the loaf of bread my mother baked. Always spread with
butter. His father had been a dairy farmer, so we always used
butter. My father would say, "May I cut some bread for you?"
and my sister and Mother and I would laugh because things
always worked out the same. He cut the heel for himself, the
next slice for my mother, and my sister and I fought over the
next two slices, about who got the tallest.

Spring comes earlier in Jackson than in Columbia. The
hyacinths Ward planted just after we moved in are poking up
around the front door. The daffodils on the empty lot north are
beginning to become a bed of white and yellow. I see new
bursts of leaves every morning. And I know that the light inside
the house will become darker for all the trees around us. "You'll
be surprised at how dark it will get in here," Ward told me this
morning at breakfast, when I commented upon seeing new leaf
growth on the oaks.

I knead the bread, push in with the heels of my hands,
and fold over what's under my fingers. I scatter some more
flour, turn the loaf and push again, fold, push, turn—the tenor,
the baritone, and my father all very near.

Movin' to Martin

You decide to move to Martin, Tennessee. Tom, your college graduate son, drives there with his dad to check things out and comes back to where you're moving from and says: "I can see why you two might like it. But I wouldn't want to live there." So he doesn't, but you do.

In Martin, Tennessee, you know nearly everybody. In a town of eight thousand it doesn't take long to get acquainted. At the lumberyard you discover that the grandfatherly man who's been helping you all these months has the word "junior" in his name and, now that you've heard him referred to that way, you too decide to call him junior. You'd heard he was a crusty fellow, but you discover he isn't at all, and, as a matter of fact, might go as far as to make a house call to see that the lumber you get is really the lumber you need.

You learn about trash and recycling. That Wednesday afternoon and Saturday mornings are the days you take your cans and newspapers to the recycling center. And that Friday morning is when the garbage truck comes through your neighborhood to collect.

You discover that the office is four minutes from your house, not the former fifteen, and that if you tell somebody, "I'll be there in five minutes," you actually will be there in five minutes because that's all the longer it takes to get anywhere in Martin, Tennessee.

Your phone bills double. That's because all the people you used to see or call with a local call now are long-distance. You check in with them regularly because many of these people

26

can't understand, altogether, why you'd leave a town of two-hundred thousand to move to a tiny place they can't find on a map of the U.S. and can barely find on a state map of Tennessee.

More than that, they can't understand why you would want to leave the home of Big Red and its seventy-six-thousand screaming fans decked out in red—red western hats, red polyester suits (some men where I came from still wear these), red boots, red and white plastic rain ponchos, red wind socks hanging from porch roofs, and red vans with the special horn installation that plays "There Is No Place Like Nebraska" every time you start to honk. They can't understand why you would want to leave all that and move to the land of the Big Orange. The big what? And if they could see the size of the football stadium in Martin, Tennessee, they would not understand even more.

In Martin, Tennessee, you buy groceries at Excel, E.W. James, Big Star, or drive to Kroger in Union City, or, for a really big outing, drive to the new Wal-Mart in Paducah.

That's something else about Martin, Tennessee. Wal-Mart. Everything is at Wal-Mart and everybody tells you everything is at Wal-Mart. You, too, begin to find everything at Wal-Mart.

By now, both your grown children are used to calling you in Martin, Tennessee. Stephanie, the divinity student in Nashville, drives over to visit. You take her to Reelfoot Lake and walk along the boardwalk. You check out the visitors center for what should be the biggest treat of all. But, the earthquake simulator is out of order. You go eat a catfish dinner anyway. And, when on Monday you report on this weekend outing to your colleague at the office, he says with admiration and a hint of teasing, "Some northerners have been known to take two whole months to recover from a catfish dinner."

By now you begin to think the color orange may have a few redeeming qualities. And while you haven't tossed out your red sweaters, your red umbrella, your red mittens, your red stocking cap, your red anorak, your red socks, or any of your red plastic dishes, you begin to warm to the color orange and you begin, cautiously, to look at Wal-Mart for anything—tasteful—in orange.

And Tom, the one who said he wouldn't want to live here, is back in Nebraska, living in fact, in the town in which he grew up, a fraction of an inch on the map from his old high school. He calls. But you're not there. You see the blinking light on the answering machine, and punch the button to play.

"Maggie," the voice says. It takes about half a beat, but you recognize the disguise. "Hey, Maggie. This is Buddy down at Buddy's Lawn and Garden. We got them thar tulips for ya. Ready to put 'em in. You just give us a call, honey."

And you crack up laughing and hit the save button and listen again. He's about got it right. But it's that last word that really gets you. Never in a million years in Nebraska would you hear anyone, except in the most married, bonded relationship, call anybody "honey." But in Martin, Tennessee, this way of talking is becoming familiar and—at your age and station in life, and you can't believe you're think this—you begin to think you might enjoy this reference—occasionally. You listen through the message again, and once more crack up as Tom says, "Just give us a call, honey."

MARGRETHE AHLSCHWEDE teaches at the University of Tennessee at Martin. Her stories and poems have appeared in journals such as *Prairie Schooner, South Dakota Review, Tampa Review*, and *Sou'wester*.

Kemmer Anderson

The Covenant

Walking through sweet pea vines and Queen Anne's Lace,
my wife gathers Spring City wildflowers in
a mason jar while I remember when
my father stood on this road with a face
turned toward a Sussex pasture found
here in Rhea County as the dairy cow
headed to the barn. I watch Martha now
kneel to mark daffodil blades that surround
and border this field deeded in a plan
typed by farm hands in my grandfather's law
office where I learned the words I saw
in a covenant between land and man.
At harvest I hold this woman, this earth,
this marriage through seasons of death and birth.

KEMMER ANDERSON is an English teacher at the McCallie School.
He has published two chapbooks of poetry, *Poem Sightings at Hunting
Island* and *A Compass Reading for Ithaca*. He and his wife Martha live
on Signal Mountain, at Running Hook Farm.

Vivian Cullum Anderson

The Homeplace

I thought there would be ghosts in this old house
when all I loved in childhood were no more.

I thought there would be a step upon the stair,
    a door would softly close behind an unseen form;
    that there would be a presence in a room
    a tenuous hovering nearness by my side
    in winter,
    when snow sifts over the walk
    and wind keens coldly through the ancient trees.

There are no ghosts here on winter days,
and leaping flames at night warm heart and room.

But, ah, when spring extends her tender hand,
    bud-tipped fingers holding balmy hours,
    then spirits do appear.

My father leans upon his hoe —
sunlight streams through windows
lighting up my mother's face.

My brother swings me in his arm again,
    and I a child, am one with bird and cloud.

Yesterday was winter and all was quiet and still.
Today spring's gentle spirits roam this house.

VIVIAN CULLUM ANDERSON lives on her family's homeplace near
Nashville, which has shrunk to 3 acres from its original 5. She is a
member of the Deer Lake Writers' Workshop.

Jan Barnett

Going Through the Smokies

I love your work — very powerful.
Jan Barnett

Fred watched every move I made while we waited in the pickup, and once we got inside the clinic, the whole waiting room could hear him telling what I'd done last night. I think that's why they took me on back to be examined. My sister Nell says she has to wait for two hours sometimes before she gets to go back and see the doctor.

The nurse wanted to know right off how long I'd been going through the change of life. I told her I didn't know, that I'd been having hot flashes for about a year.

A few minutes after that, a young girl walked in with what the nurse wrote down. "I'm Dr. Shelley," she said, "I'm new at the clinic." She said for me to relax, they'd have to do a pelvic exam before she could give me hormones.

The nurse had already put my feet in the stirrups. Dr. Shelley talked up a storm while she poked around inside me. Did I raise a big garden? Did I live in the south end of the county? Things like that. Then when the examination was over she said, "You can get dressed and someone will bring you down to my office."

She was setting behind her desk, still smiling, and wanted to know if I'd like some coffee. I said I would. Then she said, "Mrs. Burke, if you could, I'd like for you to tell me about your emotional state for the last few weeks."

I looked at her kind of funny, so she said, "Your husband seems awfully concerned. Could you just tell me what happened last night? And why?"

I thought for a minute, then I said, "I guess it all goes

31

back to me deciding to learn to drive."

I told Dr. Shelley about my niece Beth and how we had walked out to the field at the back of the house to look the cressie greens over. The sun was shining real clear that day, and the Easter flowers was crisp and pretty the way they are before the weather scars them up. Rufus, this little boy from across the road, was chasing his old shepherd dog through the field. I told him he was tromping the greens all to pieces, to go play in the yard.

We stopped in front of Fred's mother's little house that sets over to the edge of the field. "It looks bigger in the sun," Beth said. "Now that it's empty, what're you going to do with it?" Fred's mother passed away the first of the year.

"I don't know," I said. "Maybe we ought to ask sister Nell. She seems to know everything else."

Beth wanted to know what was wrong.

"Don't pay any attention to me," I said. "It's what Nell was mouthing about on the phone this morning. She claimed one of her neighbors bought his new wife a car. Said he wouldn't even buy his wife that died a spool of crochet thread. Said the first wife would have been afraid to even ask to learn to drive. She was throwing it at me. She might as well have said that's what Fred would do if I died."

Beth answered me just as sensible like, "Why, Aunt Lisbeth, why don't you learn to drive and just show Aunt Nell?"

I said I was too old.

"No you're not," she said. "I'll bet if you wanted Uncle Fred to give you driving lessons, he would. Just go ahead and ask him."

Bless Beth's heart. Nothing do her but move back to Tennessee after she graduated from college. My brother moved her and the rest of his family to Illinois when she was in the second grade. Now she's got a dandy job in a museum over at the college.

Fred says she's one of the straightest girls he's even seen. She's forever more asking him about his rabbit beagles. I thought for sure he'd pitch a fit when he found out she'd been petting his dogs, but he didn't say a word. Fred says it ruins a hunting dog to pet it. He never would let Tom play with them.

Tom's our son that went to Vietnam. Didn't even wait for the draft. Said he'd put in his time and then go to college on the GI bill. But two months before his enlistment was up, another boy in his outfit stepped on a grenade and a piece of metal hit Tom and messed up his right leg so that the doctors had to amputate it. That was three years ago. I don't know what I'd have done without Beth.

Tom was the only child we had. I miscarried with the other two. Fred was so hurt over what happened to Tom, that to this day he still won't talk about it. I rode all the way to Walter Reed Hospital and back without him saying a word to me.

He wanted Tom to move back here and put a trailer down in the field, but Tom said no. He married this little nurse who took care of him in the hospital. Her daddy's an engineer in a big airplane plant down there in Florida where they live. Tom's going to college and working at the airplane plant part time.

Fred used to be more talkative when people come around. Sister Nell says, "How do you expect anybody to feel welcome with him setting there all mulled up with his face red as a pickled beet?" She said that once in front of Beth, and Beth said, "Shame on you, Auntie Nell. He's just shy."

I think Nell just calls to see what she can find out. She's forever more asking me about Tom's wife. Tom's wife puts me in mind of Beth. She asked me once if I minded not driving.

Not driving didn't used to bother me. I worked at the garment factory before I was married, and we rode the work bus. All the girls in the mountains did. And the men, too. Fred's always took me wherever I needed to go. I know a lot of women my age who don't drive. Nell drives, but her sorry husband's too drunk to take her any place.

Fred is a little backward, and he can be hateful as the devil, but he's never knocked Tom and me around the way Daddy did my brothers and Mommy and us girls. I'll take backward over beating any day.

I know Nell says Fred's tight as the bark on a tree. I can just hear her. But it's nothing but jealousy because we have a little money in the bank and don't have to borrow all the time. Anything Nell can use to get in a dig, she'll do it. One day she pulled one of my living room curtains back and wanted to know if Fred was ever going to let me change the faded things. I told Beth after she left that I was glad Fred was saving.

Beth said, "Now Aunt Lisbeth, you deserve money for little extras. All you have to do is believe it and Uncle Fred will come around."

So the next time we went to Johnson City to the Kmart, I decided to get six rolls of blue crochet thread for a tablecloth I was making. I waited until Fred was looking for the motor oil they had on sale and slipped off to crafts and hid the thread down under some other stuff in the buggy until we got up to the register. I'd never done that before. Fred's mother drew a little pension, and she always paid for my thread. I've been using thread she left when she died.

Fred didn't say anything until we got out the door. Then he set in. "What did you need that mess for? You've got them damned crochet pieces all over the house already. I told you I was trading trucks." He always pays cash when he buys a new truck.

I said, "I deserve a little something."

He started braying, "Who do you think pays the bills? And keeps a roof over your head? God Amighty!"

I knew if I didn't say anything else, he'd simmer down. So I kept quiet, and when we got home I put the thread out of sight.

I started crocheting when Tom went to Vietnam. It made me a nervous wreck to set in front of the television listening to what was going on over there, so Fred's mother said why didn't I take up crocheting. At first my hands were so awkward, I thought I'd never make the chain stitch. But I kept on, and the first thing you know, I had made my first pineapple section.

I made all kinds of flowers and birds and put them together with the chain stitch. Beth says they're the prettiest pieces she's ever seen. She even put some in a display over at the museum. Used to I was never happier than when my head had thought up a new pattern for my hands to make, but when Beth said that about me learning to drive, I just couldn't leave it alone.

I mentioned to Fred that everybody was saying that I ought to learn to drive.

He said, "You'll have to get somebody besides me to teach you. Good God Amighty!"

Beth said not to worry, she'd do it. But she liked to never have got me in the driver's seat. Then I was afraid to turn the key in the ignition. It took me forever to get to where I could start the engine without making that screeching noise. My hands felt more awkward than when I was learning to make the chain stitch. It just didn't seem right that I was about to drive Beth's pretty little blue Maverick. That first time I took my foot off the brake and pressed down on the gas pedal, I had the funniest feeling like I was letting something loose besides the car.

We stayed in the driveway a month, me driving out to the road then backing up to the shed where Fred keeps his truck parked. I'd do this over and over. Beth's not married, so she'd come by just about every evening while Fred was working second shift. I couldn't believe none of the time, I was actually driving. Thank goodness her car's an automatic. I can't imagine what driving a straight shift'd be like.

Rufus saw us and come over. He lives with his grandparents because the man his mommy married didn't want him. He asked me to let him get in the back seat while I was prac-

ticing in the driveway. I said, "Ok, but you've got to be still."
He set back there just as quiet as could be and watched everything through these glasses he wears that make his eyes look
enlarged. But I had to have him get out the evening Beth wanted me to drive up the road.

He started snubbing and crying and kicking gravel, so I
run in the house and grabbed some of Fred's peppermint sticks
to give him. I couldn't stand to hurt his feelings. He reminds me
of Tom at that age. But I was afraid of having a wreck and hurt-
ing him. Fred's fussed about him ever since he set fire to his
granddaddy's smokehouse. He said Rufus might come over and
try to burn us out. I think it was an accident, that Rufus was
just playing with matches.

When I was finally able to pacify him and pull out on the
road, first thing here come this pickup. I wanted to stop, but
Beth said, "Keep going, you're doing fine." I must've drove for
a mile or more before she had me pull into McIntosh's driveway
and turn around. Bill and his wife come out and waved, and I
thought their eyes would pop out when they saw me behind the
wheel. I wished Nell could see me.

I worked up the nerve to go a little faster. The needle on
the speedometer was laying smack in the middle of twenty.
Beth was so tickled she said, "Aunt Lisbeth, I have an idea.
Why not sell Uncle Fred's mother's house and take the money
to buy you a car? Wouldn't a tiny little house like that be easy
to move?" She thought somebody might want it for an artist's
studio because of the picture window in the front.

"Well, we're not using it for anything," I said.

I didn't say I'd talk to Fred. But while I was waiting for
him to get home from work, I thought about all the time I spent
taking care of his mother that last year after her legs gave out
on her. It was all I could do to lift the poor old thing. I just about
wore myself out trying to make sure Fred got his meals on time
while I was taking his mother something to eat and helping her
to the bathroom and giving her a bath. I believe if he'd been the
one to clean that poor woman, she'd have rotted.

Then I thought about what a good provider Fred's been and how nice our brick ranch is that he built where his mother's old log house used to set, and how I could get by without driving. Still, when he got home, I was almost busting I was so anxious to mention buying me a car.

He wanted to know if buying me a car was Beth's idea. I said it was. "You tell her," he said, "That I'm not buying you no car to get out and cripple yourself or somebody else up and have them sue me for everything I own. You lost your mind? God Amighty! The money from Maw's house is going in the bank!"

He stubbed around the bedroom taking his pants off to get ready for bed. Then he wanted to know if the Smokies had settled in my head. Everybody around here calls the change of life the Smokies on account of this woman that went to a doctor in Knoxville, and he asked her if she'd been through the menopause, and she said, no, but she'd been through the Smokies.

I said I was sleeping in the other room. I do that sometimes when I'm burning up. I've never had such a sweat since I started through the change.

Then I walked out on the back porch and set there and looked out in the field toward the little house. Seems like the night being real quiet and still made me even more aggravated. I felt like things would have been better if it had been thundering and lightening.

I felt that something sort of like that stuff that comes out of volcanoes was trying to make its way out of my skin. And the next thing I knowed I was heading for the shed. I snatched Fred's flashlight he keeps by the door and found the kerosene can. It was about half full. I figured it'd do, but I had to go back in the kitchen for the key and some matches. I could hear Fred snoring from the other end of the house.

I've heard people talk about throwing stuff around like holy water. That's what I did. I sloshed kerosene all over Fred's mother's old recliner and her hide-a-bed. Then I ripped one of the curtains off a window and walked out on the front step and lit it and threw it back in on the recliner.

It wasn't long until "Whoosh!" and I knew the kerosene had caught. I walked back to the porch and watched the flames shoot out through the windows and the doors. It kind of reminded me of a jack-o-lantern. I had left everything open except the picture window. Pretty soon it popped, and I felt kind of like something around me cracked open and I stepped out. I started to cool off. The higher them flames shot, the better I felt.

I'd started back in the house to get a sweater when I heard Rufus' granddaddy coming across the road. "Burke! Burke! Wake up! You're on fire! Get out of there!" Rufus was with him.

Fred was still putting on his pants when he pitched out on the porch. He's a heavy sleeper. He saw Rufus, thought he'd set the fire and started cussing and threatening the old man for everything he could lay his tongue to. I don't think he even saw me.

I slipped back in the house and went in the bedroom and pushed a chest up against the door. I could hear Fred hooking up the water hose, still cussing every breath. But it was too late. The little house was a goner.

It was way up in the morning when he came banging on the door wanting to know why the hell I'd locked it. I could tell he still hadn't figured out what'd happened. So I said real quiet like to him, "I'm the one that set that fire." And then I didn't say another word. I just let him rant on till daylight.

Dr. Shelley laughed so hard, I didn't think she'd ever finish writing out my prescription. Finally she handed it to me and said, "This is for hormones. They should take care of the hot flashes." Then she started laughing again, "Let me know if you feel like burning any more houses down. I can increase the dosage."

I took the prescription and looked at it and thought for

a minute. Then I handed it back to her. "No thank you," I said.

JAN BARNETT is a native and lifetime resident of Unicoi County. She left a position in accounting three years ago to pursue her dream of being a writer.

Tamara M. Baxter

Black Dark

Mama makes me go through Mr. Fred's holler, and it black dark and me not able to see my hand in front of my eyes and night sounds coming at me ever which way. Owls screeching inside my head and feet swishing right by me in the leaves and me not seeing a thing, not knowing what it is. Mama doesn't know what it is like to run through bushes at night, brier vines clawing at my coat sleeves and possum vines trying to hang me by the neck like running into a clothes line in the dark, and stepping into holes I can't see.

But Mama says I must go through Mr. Fred's holler in black dark again if she needs to send me for help when the baby comes. I am almost nine now, she says, a big boy, not like two summers ago when Mama's pains came during the night hard and fast and Mama sent me to get Mr. Fred to come and drive her to the hospital. That's because Daddy is never home much. Daddy plays pinochle in the back of Shakey's pool room.

Mama says she's going to get dynamite someday and blow up Depot Street, one pool room after another. She's going to blow up all the beer joints and pool rooms where men go to hide from their families. She's going to blow them one at a time and laugh while the whole street blazes to glory.

And what about Daddy?, I say. Are you going to blow him up too?

And Mama says, *Yes*, sadly. *Blowing all of it up. The dim rooms, the men who laugh with cigarettes shaking in the corners of their mouths, their eyes fixed on a deck of cards, their hands always readying for a mug.* Mama shakes her head and says, *They plant not, neither do they reap.*

But mostly it is because of the money on the tables which can't ever be spent on ten pounds of potatoes, or a sack of sugar or coffee, or pretty things for the house, but because the money must always be spent on beer and more cards and laughing. Mama says playing the cards makes men hate their women and children and their homes, and the drinking makes men kill their unborn babies, like two years ago. So, she's going to blow it all up. And, also, I must go through the holler in black dark if need be, and I say, Yes, Mama.

Mama irons clothes beside the kitchen sink where the light comes in the little window. Her belly is big and moves itself against the edge of the ironing board. The light bulb in the kitchen is busted in the socket. There is no light and Daddy does not fix it. And sometimes when Mama is ironing, Grandmama Caine comes knocking at the front door with a brown sack in her arms.

Grandpa Caine brings Grandmama in his pickup and parks beside the great big bank in front of our house which sits on the road like Humpty Dumpty, and I can look down from the porch and see the rusted roof of his Ford. He sits and waits in the hot truck on Grandmama to get done with her visiting. Says he won't claim a daughter who runs off to marry a no-account, who breaks her parents' hearts. He has never been inside this house or in the other place we lived before. That was a little shingle house near the river.

I go out and sit in the truck with him sometimes while Mama and Grandmama talk. Grandpa Caine rubs my head with his big hand and says, *How's my boy?* Then he reaches way down in his overalls pocket and pulls up some change, fingering through a mess of washers and oats to find me a nickel. And I say, Grandpa Caine, could I buy me a flashlight with this nickel at Susong's Store? Grandpa laughs at me. I will not tell him I am afraid of the dark.

And Grandmama Caine comes in with her brown poke rattling cans of green beans, chow-chow and bread-and-butter pickles. She puts them on the table one by one out of the poke

41

saying, *Here's a little something from me and your Pa. And here's a can of pumpkin for pies.*

Grandmama Caine never looks at Mama. She sits and rubs her finger in a hole in the yellow checked table cloth. She asks Mama if she's put up much canning, and Mama says, *No, the garden isn't much this year.* Grandmama says she knows it's because Daddy doesn't help keep the garden up or plant a decent stand of beans and corn to begin with.

After while Grandmama says she's heard a woman talking at the store. Mr. Fred may be getting shed of us, Daddy doesn't do his part on the farm anymore. Mr. Fred has put the word out for new renters. Mama runs the iron over the clothes the same as if she didn't hear.

Then, Mama whispers to the ironing board that Daddy was different before the war, before he learned bad things overseas in places not fit to live, in trenches, outside in the cold with the noise of bombs and bullets blasting inside his mind, in a place called the Bulge. *He's okay when he's not drinking. He's as good as any man when he's sober.* Grandmama says, *Huh! Your man comes off bad blood. He's no account like the rest of his people.* When we hear the red truck pull away from the bank, Mama cries up at the ceiling. *God, why have you forsaken me?*

I count Daddy home every night beside the open window with crickets and tree frogs screaming in the dark. They scream without stopping until morning because they are afraid. As long as they can answer themselves, they know they are alive in the dark.

I hear myself count to sixty over and over until he comes. Daddy's junk car rolls in slow beside the bank, and he parks in the worn, muddy ruts. His car door shuts loud and the tree frogs stop screaming for a second of silence. Then, his big boots stomp up the plank steps against the bank. Then his boots stomp along the short walk Mama made from a sack of concrete Mr. Fred gave her to keep the mud from tracking in. Daddy stops and pees in the pretty-by-nights Mama planted along the front porch. She is proud of her flowers, and in the evening she waters them, and holds their little chins in her fingers and smiles.

Sometimes Daddy gets us out of bed in the night. He wants the lights on. He wants food on the table. *Where is the meat?*, he says. *A man needs meat. It is almost morning*, Mama says back. *Go to sleep. You'll wake the boy.* She sees me peeping out of my room in the dark. The baby churns under Mama's gown. *Bitch*, he says. I see his hand go back and hear it crack like a whip against Mama's face. She screams, *Get behind the door! Behind the door!*

I have a hidey-hole in the corner behind my big oak door. I have wooden spools for soldiers and tin cans for my fort. And there is a big crack where the hinges are when the door is opened back into the corner, and that is my spy hole. I have a rope that Grandpa gave me out of his truck. Inside my hidey-hole, I tie the rope around the doorknob that is white and smooth as a hen's egg. Then I tie it round a big nail, as big as Daddy's fingers, hammered in the floor. But this is for the day.

For night, I put the rope around the nail and then around my hands and hold tight. Behind the door, I listen to Daddy's boots walking crooked across the floor boards. The living room light comes to the crack along the hinges and I can hear Mama screaming, *Get behind the door!* and I can hear my body screaming inside like tree frogs. Inside my body comes Mama's screaming, then she does not scream anymore. Through my spy hole, I see the soles of Mama's feet.

Daddy's boots stomp toward the door, then in the crack comes his big eye, nervous like a horse's. He tries to see into the dark, but his big body blocks the light. Something burns inside my head, and the rope burns my hands. After while, his boots stomp away, but they come back fast. His eye is back again, and then comes his breath through the crack like rotten potatoes. He pulls hard on the loose doorknob, and it rattles like bolts in a can. The rope jerks through my fingers burning hot. He says, *Come out of there boy!* The side of his sweaty face is flashing in the living room light. I pull the rope tighter. Thank you God.

Thank you for the dark behind this door.

I love you Mama. I love you. When I grow up I'm going to buy you that candy dress, red and white striped in Powell and Sandel's, the one you stop and gaze at through the window and lick your lips for. The sandals, too. White patent leather you called them. I will have money then, lots of money, and we will shop on Saturday morning. After the dress, we will go the Corner Drug, and I will order two chocolate sodas the way we like them in tall glasses with straws. We will sit on the stools and swivel round and round, even if the drugstore man shakes his finger and says, *No*.

* * *

Mr. Fred says we must not mess up his car. It is a new '57 Plymouth with grey inside like touching velvet cloth. I promise him the baby will not mess up his car, if only he will please hurry.

His shirt hangs out of his pants. His eyes come in angry slits like a dog about to growl when he sees Daddy snoring across the bed, and Mama lying in a round, wet spot on the wooden floor.

Mr. Fred puts me in the front and Mama lies on the back seat. We start up the road, and Mama screams, *The baby is coming. Now*, she says, *Now!* Mr. Fred pulls into his own driveway. He blows his car horn, and then Misses Fred is standing under the yellow bulb on the back porch. Misses Fred goes inside the house, and then she comes to the car through the yellow light with something in her hand. Towels.

Mama cries in the back seat. I cannot see her face. Mr. Fred tells me to go behind the car and stand. Misses Fred gets into the back of the car and after awhile she gets out again. She takes the soft bundle of towels toward the yellow light in front of her like a plate of hot biscuits. There is no sound of screaming in the dark, not even the tree frogs. Mr. Fred's car is shiny slick behind, and when I put my fingers on it, I can feel Mama crying in the bumper.

I love you Mama. When I grow up, we will have a house

44

much bigger than this one of Mr. Fred's. It will be bright white like blazing sun with big round poles to hold up the porch. We will live along the river and have rocking chairs on the porch like in magazines, and we will rock in the chairs where breezes will come to fan our faces in the afternoon. We will have a rug on our floor, and plenty of pretty curtains for our house. We will have a better car than Mr. Fred's with velvet seats, and a good flashlight so I will not be afraid to walk through the holler in the dark ever, ever again.

✿ ✿ ✿

Mr. Fred's holler is shaped like Daddy's car, and when we drive through it, the morning sun on the windshield looks like a spider's web. Mama says that it is dangerous. She says the whole glass could bust out in our faces before we could say jack-in-the-box. Daddy says, *Shut up*, around the cigarette in his mouth. Mama gets quiet, mostly because her belly hurts and she is bent over in the front seat. She jerks the handle so hard the door flies open on Mr. Fred's curve, and Daddy grabs her in. *For God's sake, lock that door*, he says. *Daddy goes too fast*, she says back. And then Mama starts the crying again.

Daddy says we must have the funeral ourselves. There is no money for a blue casket with a white lining like Mama wants. No money for the fancy undertakers. *They smile at you like they are friends, but they only want money*, he says. *Two years ago them undertakers took half the tobacco crop. Yes*, Mama whispers back, *and still no rock to mark his grave, to mark his coming and going.*

When we get to Susong's store, two men are standing on the porch. One is Mr. Akers of the Greeneville Mill who grinds Mama's corn. A great noisy machine makes the corn meal. The cobs go in a metal mouth on one side, and yellow meal flies out the spout on the other side. I like to feel it snowing though my fingers into the sack. Another man I do not know is drinking a dope with his hand on his hip. They stare at us like we are pictures in a book and do not speak.

Daddy pumps the gas and goes inside to pay. He walks around them like trees. He comes out with wooden crates under his arms and dangling off his hands. He puts the crates in the trunk, and ties the lid with twine to keep them in. Through the window, he hands Mama a B. C. Powder and a chocolate dope, the kind she likes. *Didn't you get the boy one too?* she says. Mama hands me her chocolate dope across the seat. It tastes grainy and bitter like Epsom Salts around the rim.

Across the road, the children are in the school behind the big windows that go from top to bottom and have many squares. *When we settle in at Mr. Fred's, I will send the boy to Walker's School*, I heard Mama say to Daddy when we moved in Mr. Fred's little brown house. At Walker's School I will learn to make A's like Indian tee-pees, and S's like snakes, and T's like crosses, and D's like a waxing moon, and C's like a moon in wane. Mama tells me that is how I will know my letters, and then I will make them words. Mama shows me how to draw the snakes and crosses and the moons with a pencil on a grocery bag.

Daddy says there is no need for learning words. *No need to send the boy to Walker's School, or any school. Woman, you want to shame me by sending the boy to school? Look. I lived through a war, dammit. I thought I was dead a thousand times. Don't you make light of me!*

But the boy is almost nine, she says back. *You know how to read a deck of cards, let the boy learn to read books.*

And now I will not go to Walker's School. We must leave the little house that sits like Humpty Dumpty on our bank, and I wave out the car to the children who read behind the windows.

The children do not know me, or that I can count to sixty. Mama says I must not tell Daddy that I can draw the numbers along the edge of the magazine with pretty houses, or say them in my mind.

When we are driving on the road I try to count the trees that pass by the car windows. They go too fast. But I can count the seven houses on the windey road by Granny Lewis Creek, and the two at Tilson's Gap, little houses with flowers by the porch. One house has a clothesline with overalls and blue jeans walking on the wind. I count a big man and six strapping boys living on this clothesline.

After the mountain there are no more houses to count, and so I watch the road run by the rusty hole in the floorboard, blurry, like going round and round. I cannot stop looking at it. *The boy is sick*, Mama says. *He's had nothing but a bite of pone and milk since morning.* Daddy says we will be at Aunt Spivey's by supper. There is only money for gas.

Aunt Spivey is on the front steps wiping her hands on the bottom of her apron when we drive up her little road. Her face is figuring out our car.

We can go back and get the stuff later, Daddy tells Mama. *When I can borrow a truck. Aunt Spivey will let us put it in her barn until we get a place.*

The bundle is wrapped round and round with towels, tight, like a big white egg. Mama says, *Hand the baby up. I will carry it myself.* It smells like a ripe mushmellon. I shake my head *No*. Daddy says he will come around and get it for her.

Aunt Spivey comes to the car wringing her hands on the bottom of her apron. *She leans half-way into the car. Laws me. What is this?* she says. Her gums are pinkey-red when she opens her mouth to look at our baby wrapped up like an egg in Misses Fred's towels.

❅ ❅ ❅

There is a feast of food on Aunt Spivey's table. Streaky meat and beans, sliced tomatoes, fried potatoes with onions. And lots of buttermilk. There is a blackberry cobbler with warm milk for afters. Aunt Spivey says, *Laws, I'd have cooked more if I'd a knowed you was coming.*

Mama does not eat. She sits beside the window watching up the hill where Daddy hammers the boards together from the wooden crates out of the trunk. Aunt Spivey says it is best for Mama to rest. She puts Mama's feet into a pan of steamy water to ward off cold. Aunt Spivey says she will bind Mama's belly tight with strips of white cloth she tears from a sheet to make her go back right. Aunt Spivey rubs lard on the side of Mama's face that is purple, and rubs around her eye that is swelled shut. Her brown fingers are like knobby twigs of kindling. *Laws have mercy, why put up with a man like that?* She shakes her fist at the window where Daddy is framed like a picture on the hill with the wooden box and his shovel digging. *If he wasn't my kin, I'd of lawed him myself,* she says.

Mama says to Aunt Spivey that Daddy can not help himself. Her voice is the same as when the two men from the Susong's store came and found Daddy on the bed asleep, and Mr. Akers jerked him up while the one I do not know punched into his belly. And Mama said, *Stop. Stop. He can not help it. He doesn't mean to do it. Leave us alone.* Daddy was asleep and could not feel their fists, so the two men dropped him on the floor like a rag. They looked hard at Mama with questions in their eyes, then went away.

There has been a storm, but only the trees are raining now. Mama starts the crying again. *Won't the water get to my lamb?* she says. Aunt Spivey rubs a white cloth with lard to wrap the baby in and Mama hushes.

I love you Mama. When I am grown up and have lots of money, I will buy you a blue box with a white lining for our baby, the way you like it. And I will also buy a rock for our other baby to mark its coming and going. And I will go to Walker's School and make words of the crosses and moons. We will sit on the porch swing of a late afternoon and read my words with your fingers under them, and swing and swing.

* * *

Daddy cannot sleep here. Aunt Spivey held him out with her broom handle across the door like a gun. He would not cross her path. Aunt Spivey says that she is ashamed to claim Daddy as kin, and that is why he is gone. I have never seen Daddy afraid of anyone before, but he did not cross the old woman with her broom-gun across the door. Daddy shouts inside to Mama that he will come back and fetch her when he has found a place. Aunt Spivey tells him he will find his place in hell. He goes away and we hear his car drive over the rocks into the dark.

Mama will sleep in Aunt Spivey's big bed. Mama lies atop the bed as cold and still as a chunk of stove wood. I can see her eyes jump back and forth under the clearness of her lids. One side of Mama's face is white like a plate, and the other side is like the rotten belly of a cucumber. Aunt Spivey tucks a pieced quilt of many scraps around Mama.

Aunt Spivey says Mama is sick because she has bled too much. That is why she is limp as a dishrag. That is why her head rolls around on the pillow like a marble in a dishpan. Aunt Spivey says she can cure the fever and stop the blood. It is a gift she has. She will use cold rags and willow bark tea and many prayers.

Mama is beautiful and still like the marble lady who lies atop her grave at the New Ebenezer Presbyterian Church. Mama says the marble lady belonged to a rich family who can afford such trifles. Amanda Wingfield Evans, the grave says.

When Daddy is not home and we must walk to Susong's Store, Mama takes me across the road and up the hills, and we walk among the dead people and read their graves. Mama puts her fingers on the words and says them out loud, *Here Lies Amanda Wingfield Evans, Beloved Wife of Jacob Evans.* I do not like to see the cold, marble lady asleep atop her own grave, but I like to read the words.

It is really our dead baby buried near the fence row along the graveyard that Mama comes to see. He is marked with a little pile of rocks and a peach sapling that Mama planted on his head.

And now Mama is like the marble lady, quiet and still, and Aunt Spivey sits beside her with the cold rags and her tonic in a snuff glass. Aunt Spivey is very old. She wears dresses old-woman long that slosh about her ankles. Her skin is yellow like old wallpaper and her voice does not sing the words like Mama does. She is reading her cures from the Book of Ezekiel. When she sucks in and out with her mouth open, her breath smells like turpentine. But she has twinkly eyes, and she is good to help Mama who is not even her blood kin. It is Daddy who belongs to her family, her great-nephew on her brother's side.

Aunt Spivey will sleep sitting in her chair beside Mama's bed, and I will sleep on a pallet of quilts Aunt Spivey made for me on the living room floor. My pallet smells like Aunt Spivey's cedar chest. She sets out a clean paint bucket if I need to make water in the night. I have a good ham biscuit I saved in my pocket to eat under the covers.

A kerosene lamp beside Mama's bed licks its flame against the dark window. It licks and licks at the black night coming in the window, and only the lamp's dim light to hold back all that darkness. I want to tell my Mama and Aunt Spivey to guard the lamp because I am afraid of the dark coming into the room. They will only say hush now and go to sleep. It will be morning soon.

But outside the tree frogs are silent, and I am afraid before morning comes the dark will push in through the window.

TAMARA M. BAXTER is an Associate Professor of English at Northeast State Technical Community College in Blountville. Her stories have been published in over a dozen literary journals and anthologies, including *Artemis*, *Wellspring*, and the *Nightshade Reader*. This story won the 1994 Harriette Arnow Award for fiction.

Linda Behrend-Akard

Remembering Freddie

For Elizabeth
Frida Behrend
Akard

He said the mountains and trees in Upper East Tennessee reminded him of the Black Forest in his native Germany. He came here in the late 1920s, answering an ad in a New York newspaper for a German-English stenographer at a plant "near Johnson City, Tennessee."

The Rayon plants were just getting started in Elizabethton and he came here to work, not knowing where or how far away Johnson City was. I asked him once about leaving home and family to come to a foreign land, and he told me that everyone at that time thought, if only they could get to America, they could start a new life—that it was "the land of opportunity." It was for him. . .

He said he had only about $13 in his pocket when he got off the boat in New York City. He only got to come because his friend's uncle died after the two of them had already booked passage on a ship to the States. He came in place of the uncle and went to work wrapping packages in a publishing house/ book distribution warehouse in New York City. Then he got the job working for the Bemberg plant and came to Elizabethton. He came here, to this "beauty spot" in Tennessee, to make a life—and spent his life, giving back as much as his adopted country gave him.

He worked in the corporate offices at the Rayon plants in Elizabethton for 25-30 years, until the company changed hands and the "New York bunch" who took over decided to clean out the front office. And this man, who was nearing retirement age, went to the publisher of the local newspaper

51

and said, "I want to go to work for you." He had been associated with a news agency years before in Germany; now he went "on the beat" for the *Elizabethton Star*, covering City Council meetings, sheriff and police reports, wrecks, fires, local news— you name it, he was there. I know—I went on a lot of those stories with him.

I am remembering Fred W. Behrend, my father— "Freddie," as most people called him. I don't remember thinking he was different when I was small. The first time probably was when I was in first grade and one of the boys went to get his mother (she worked in the cafeteria) to come and look at me in the lunchroom because I was half-German. Being half-German didn't mean anything to me. I just knew that lots of people said they had trouble understanding my father when he talked. I couldn't understand that. He was just Daddy, and I didn't have any trouble understanding him.

We used to go to Knoxville a lot when I was a child (my mother was from Knoxville), and I knew all the towns and the route 11-E took through all the towns between Elizabethton and Knoxville. There was a certain corner in Greeneville; and, every time we turned that corner, Daddy would point and say, "That's where I was born!" He was pointing to the Federal Courthouse where he became a naturalized citizen of the United States of America. Citizenship and patriotism meant a lot to him, and we were taught to salute the flag and treat it with respect and to stand at attention for the Star-Spangled Banner. In later years, he asked my mother if there wasn't a song called "America, the Beautiful." When she sang "for purple mountains' majesty," he began to weep.

The mountains had been his life. Every Saturday, he was up before dawn—gone out to hike in the mountains. It was often after dark when he got home. When he went hiking, he always wore his Khaki's and, in bad weather, there were sweaters and scarves and mittens and parkas and overshoes. There was a ritual my sister and I were part of when he came back in. We got to pull off all the sweaters and parkas and scarves, etc. He would lean over and we would peel the layers off one by one.

The people in the mountains called him "the bird man." They knew him because he came week after week to walk the mountains and watch the birds and look for wildflowers and ferns. I cannot remember a time when the "bird club" was not an important part of our life. Some of my earliest memories are of TOS (Tennessee Ornithological Society) meetings in our home and the recording of the bird census for the Christmas count. Someone would read from the "official" list of birds and, as the name of each bird was intoned, members would call out "one specie—one male, two females" (or however many they had seen and identified). I remember being fascinated by the word "specie"—I had no idea what it meant. It seemed that different people said it differently. I guess that different people said it differently. I guess that was one of the first times I noticed my father's accent, although I wasn't aware that that was what it was.

I didn't know until after his death whey he got interested in wildflowers and ferns. His pastor told the story when Bear Wallow Trail in Roan Mountain State Park was dedicated to his memory. Daddy had told him that when he would go out into the mountains after my sister died, he couldn't look up—as he had for so long to watch the birds. It was then that he noticed the wildflowers and plants at ground level and began to be interested in them. This new focus became as important as his interest in birds. he sat up nights studying, visited the library, bought books, took innumerable color slides, pressed and dried specimens—always pursuing a new discovery.

It all culminated in the Roan Mountain Wildflower Tour. I remember Daddy being incensed about Wildflower Walks held in the Smokies each spring. He said we had just as many wildflowers in this area and probably a greater variety. So he organized a wildflower tour for our area to be held each spring. I can still remember sitting on the front porch stuffing envelopes for the mailing for that and the Naturalists' Rally, a companion gathering held each fall the weekend after labor Day. They still hold these events, my father's brainchild, and bring in speakers and volunteers from all over to present programs and lead field trips to study wildflowers, birds, plants, rocks, salamanders, trees—whatever the good Lord had put out there for our enjoyment.

Daddy knew the mountains by name, and, I dare say, had hiked over at least all the ones in East Tennessee. Roan Mountain, Jane Bald, Hump Mountain, Carvers Gap, Iron Mountain, Holston—these names were as familiar as neighbors on our street. We were always going to Roan Mountain for picnics and holidays. It was his favorite place to take visitors from out of town, too. He would always caution them in the summer to take along a sweater or jacket "because it's cool up there" due to the higher elevation. Most didn't believe him, and some didn't take his advice and learned the hard way that he knew what he was talking about.

I can remember, as a child, going to Lynn Mountain with my new little Brownie camera to hike with Daddy. They used to tell a story on me about Daddy carrying me up that mountain on his back (when I was small) and the going kept getting tougher and tougher and he couldn't seem to make any headway. He looked around to find that I was holding onto a bush.

Lynn Mountain is a mountain at the east end of town where they always put up three crosses near the top at Easter time. We always went around to the back side of the mountain, though, to climb. We would drive out to Rasor farm (sometimes Daddy would let me sit on his lap and hold the steering wheel as we went down the dirt road) and park the car and go up the mountain from that side. It was from there he went on his last hike.

I remember when he used to go off to the Roan to hike and be gone all day and often until after dark. I was always so afraid that he wouldn't come back—that something would happen. Well, this time he didn't come home. I was grown and married with children of my own and lived in another town. My mother called to say that she had just called the rescue squad to go look for him. I can't remember if the lady at Rasor farm called my mother before or after that. She called to ask, "Is Mr. Behrend going to spend the night on the mountain?" She knew his car, parked there so many times before, and became concerned when he didn't return as night came on.

She knew where he went to look for the wildflowers and led the rescue squad right to him. He had had a stroke and couldn't get up. Someone asked him how he felt, lying there with night coming on. He said he still had part of his sandwich and a piece of Hershey bar in his pocket and he ate them and just looked up and watched the stars coming out, and everything was beautiful.

The marker at Roan Mountain State Park says it all:

Fred W. Behrend, 1896-1976
"Naturalist and Lover of Roan Mountain"

LINDA BEHREND-AKARD is an east Tennessee native, educated at the University of Tennessee at Knoxville, and currently settled in Bristol. She has done newspaper work, public relations, and is now an academic librarian.

Ronna Blaser

All Your Lives At Once

Josie had met Jacob Benner in passing years ago, and when she saw him at the Nashville Book Emporium one Saturday night, he looked familiar. Josie had started stopping at the bookstore ever since she split up with Bill. She liked to wander in the aisles when she didn't have plans or didn't want to be alone in her apartment.

That night she was thumbing through *Understand Yourself: The Definitive Key to Personality.* Her friend Glenda had recommended it.

When Josie closed the book, she noticed Jacob standing nearby. He was staring at her. She was in her new white blouse and short black skirt, and she felt suddenly self-conscious, but pleased.

"Hi," he said too loudly for a bookstore. "Do you come here often?"

"Quite a bit," Josie answered. She tried to place him, but couldn't. He had black curly hair, wore jeans and a denim jacket. He wasn't really handsome, but there was something appealing about him. The dark eyes. His easy smile, The way he moved his lean body when he walked over to her.

He asked about the book she was reading. Josie handed it to him. "Self-help," he pronounced, flipping pages. Then he reached into his pocket and gave her a business card.

It read: "Jacob Arthur Benner, attorney at Law," with his address, phone and FAX number.

"Just so you know I'm not some marginal personality." He grinned. "I know we've met before, but I can't remember where, can you?"

"No. You look familiar, though."

"This isn't a good place to talk. I should tell you right away, I am a very direct person." He touched Josie's arm. "Do you want to have coffee?"

On the way to the cafe, Jacob snapped his fingers. "Now I remember," he said. "we met just after I moved to Nashville, five years ago. At a Christmas party, an arts benefit. You were with a tall guy. He had a pony tail. A music type."

"That must be it," Josie said. She worked for the Metropolitan Arts Council. She had been to every Christmas party; Bill was a musician and had always come along, too.

At the cafe, Jacob ordered coffee. Josie had tea. She told him she drank coffee only when she stayed up late to paint. She would set a canvas on an easel in her kitchen then, and paint into the night. "I love it. Though if I'm working the next day, I'm tired."

"You're lucky. I used to play guitar, read books all day, but who has time anymore?" He was an entertainment lawyer, he explained. Divorced. No children. "The job might sound glamorous. I travel for it, which is great, but with songwriters and singers there's a lot of hand holding."

Josie told him she had been with the arts Council for eight years. "I plan exhibits and help artist network. I lived with a man for four years. Bill." She hesitate, deciding whether to tell Jacob more. But she went on. "We never married, though it was terrible when we split up. Like a divorce," she said softly. "He believed monogamy wasn't a natural state."

"But monogamy is a natural state," Jacob replied brightly. "It's just not easy to find the right person." He reddened, and sipped his coffee, then looked at her seriously. "This is my situation. I've given up with the Personals. I've had my share of relationships, then stayed away from women completely. Celibate. Now I'd like to meet someone. Not just anyone." He leaned toward Josie. "But there are a thousand reasons people don't want to be involved. I like to know right away."

"You are direct." She laughed. "Do you want a resume, too?"

"I'm sorry," he said sheepishly. "I didn't mean to be pushy. My ex-wife always said I was. But the problem was she didn't want a normal life."

"That's a problem," Josie replied. Then she explained that she wanted to meet someone, too. To fall in love again, she thought dreamily, though she didn't mention love to Jacob. "But it's complicated," she said. She told him about married friends who were separating, single friends dying to get married. One friend was desperately trying to have a child, another complained she had too many. "I know couples in pre-marital counseling, post-martial counseling. People want what they don't have. And when they finally get it, they don't want it anymore."

"Too many choices." Jacob shrugged. "It's like musical partners these days." He pushed away his coffee cup. "My mother never told me life would be like this. She taught me to be polite, get a good job, and marry the first nice girl I saw. I did that. But it didn't work." He sighed. "I guess you have to make up your life as you go along."

The day after Josie had coffee with Jacob, she phoned Glenda.

"You've come to the right source," Glenda announced. "You don't want to waste your time if he doesn't have potential."

"I suppose not," Josie replied. "But I like him."

"I know a little about him. Jacob moved to Tennessee from New York. His wife left him. She joined a cult. People say he took it with great equanimity. He's abrasive, I think, but charming."

Josie had gone to lunch with Glenda just last week. They were in a women's group, too, but the group was disbanding. Three members were moving away, including Glenda.

She was getting married as well.

At lunch, Josie had asked how Glenda felt about getting married.

"Ecstatic," Glenda said. "Still, what a struggle to decide. There are no guarantees. I guess you just have to dive in. Sometimes what you're afraid of is what you want the most." She retrieved a mint from her purse and popped it into her mouth. She was a reformed smoker. "It's simple to give advice," she went on, "but you'll never get married if you keep choosing men like Bill. You have to be careful before you fall in love, to find someone who wants what you do."

"If only it were that easy," Josie sighed.

"At least that's what I did. Todd isn't perfect. But who is? I'm not looking for perfection. I won't be a prisoner of my psyche anymore."

Jacob invited Josie to dinner later that week. He lived in a townhouse. A few pieces of modern furniture and plants sat in the living room. Photographs of wildflowers hung on the walls.

They drank wine and ate spaghetti at the kitchen table which Jacob had covered with a red and white checked cloth.

He asked about Josie's paintings. She told him about her large abstract canvases splashed with color. "Though I'm not really a serious artist," she explained. She paused, because sometimes she worried she jumped from one thing to another — an artists' colony in Mexico, a bike trip in the Smoky mountains — collecting experiences, like others collected possessions. She worried she wasn't serious about anything. Not about art or work, even love. But she said to Jacob, "There isn't time for all I want to do."

"Time does run out," he agreed quietly. "For everyone."

After dinner, they went for a walk. Josie asked Jacob about his divorce.

"My ex-wife wasn't sure she wanted children," he began. "She wanted to find herself first. She started to study with the Maharishi Hawa. Then she complained I was noisy during her meditation. I tried to be quiet. I joked—'I'm from Buffalo, not Bombay.' I even agreed to raise our children to meditate. but one day she told me it didn't matter. She had gone beyond me." He frowned and clapped his hands. "She left, just like that."

"I'm sorry," Josie said, touched by the wistfulness in his voice.

It was a hot, humid night, and they strolled along a wide boulevard, by the light of a full moon. "After the divorce," Jacob continued, "I dated lots of women. Then I stopped. I realized there are tons of people in the world, a million permutations for romance. But everyone has problems." He looked at Josie. "What are yours?"

"That's starting backwards." She blushed and thought: My problem is I used to be so sure of what I wanted—an unfettered life, to be free. Now I'm not so sure. But she said, "I want a family. Bill never did; I never used to, either. There's not much time left."

"That's not a problem." Jacob grinned and draped his arm around her, kissing her. "That's a call from the soul."

They began going to dinner and movies, sometimes talking for hours. Josie looked forward to seeing him. Jacob could be abrupt and impatient, too.

On a few Saturday nights, he had complimentary tickets to a bluegrass club and Opryland. He took Josie backstage, and she met some performers. "Perks of the job," he said proudly.

She showed Jacob her paintings, which he admired. She did sketches of his face, too, drawing the gentle sweep of his chin and mouth, the dark eyes, so clear and intense they seemed to hold her.

Jacob explained to her about the intricate contracts he wrote for recording companies. Once when Josie was visiting his office, he told her, "I used to play guitar. I moved to

Nashville with the same dream everyone has. To make music, be discovered. But you give up those things if they're not meant to be. Besides, I love my work now; it suits me."

Sometimes Josie gazed at Jacob, her heart pounding. Then she would remember Glenda's words, thinking: be careful before you fall in love.

A few weeks after they met, on a rainy early fall afternoon, Jacob phoned Josie at work. He said that she had five minutes to make the most important decision of her life.

Josie had to put him on hold, other lines were ringing; but when she returned, he explained that his firm was sending him to Arizona for four days. He could bring someone along. "For free."

"But we're not married," she laughed.

"They don't care who I bring. Besides, I'm a man of honor. Or maybe there's someplace you'd rather go. Like Bali. If that comes up, I'll call, too. But Arizona is fine for now."

They stayed in a resort hotel in Phoenix, in two rooms. During the day Jacob was busy with work. Josie read by the pool. They took leisurely walks at lunch. At dinner, they toasted to their six week anniversary. Josie gave Jacob a card that she had painted with a sketch of him inside.

He gave her a small book of Buddhist quotations. "It's `tashi shopa'—auspicious circumstance—that we met," he said. His inscription read: "To Josie, who I think I am beginning to love."

That night, in his room, they kissed. But this kiss felt different to Josie. Not because of the gift or being in Arizona or because of what Jacob had written. It was as if this feeling for him had been growing inside of her all along, but she had just noticed it now. She wrapped her arms around him happy, as if she were touching a man for the first time.

After Jacob fell asleep, Josie lay in his arms. He was a man of honor, she thought, a dear man. Whatever happened between them tonight was her doing, too. She kissed his hand gently, then reproached herself, cautious. She'd had romances before; they never lasted. She thought now of all the times she had been in love. With Al Minet when she was a teenager, and his touch had felt like love. Love everlasting, she had imagined then.

There were others in college and after, a percussionist, another who had been studying pulse diagnosis. Then Bill, how she'd fallen for him. She had almost given up on love after him. Now was she falling in love with Jacob? Would she let herself? Josie sighed. What was love anyway? Could you tell by browsing, by hoping? Maybe Glenda was right, you had to let yourself fall, dive in whether you were afraid or not, like tumbling from an airplane with a parachute. Trust that the chute would open and you would sail safely through the air.

Back in Nashville, after the Arizona trip, Jacob and Josie saw each other almost every night. Always during the day when she was at work, Josie thought about him, how much she cared for him.

Once, Jacob mentioned marriage. "It might be premature," he said, "but if things continue between us like this, it's something to think about."

Josie had put her arm around him. She imagined having children with Jacob, growing old together. But then she stopped herself, afraid. She wondered if you could count on spending your life with any one person.

Jacob was scheduled to go on business trips, a few days to Dallas, then Washington, a week in Los Angeles. A complicated trail was coming up in California.

"It figures," he groaned. "Just when we're getting started. But it's my job."

The California case didn't settle as he hoped. The preparations and trial might last three months. Josie phoned him when he was away, but he was difficult to reach. He didn't have much time to call her. "The work is intense. Sometimes I don't know what day it is. I'll come home a few weekends. But we should send FAXes," he suggested. "We'll become pen pals. It will be fun."

There wasn't a facsimile machine at the Arts Council, so Josie went to the Good Neighbor Pharmacy near her apartment. She had seen a sign in the window: "Community FAX Center. Low cost sending and receiving. Free numbers."

When Josie got her FAX number, Jacob began sending messages. The pharmacist would call to let her know when transmissions arrived. Jacob sent them almost every day, on the firm letterhead. Short, informative notes. He couldn't write anything too personal because the messages were sent from work. But he signed them "Jacob Benner, I.L.U.," for I love you.

Josie sent reserved notes as well. She always drew a small sketch of two people holding hands.

At first when Jacob was away, she missed him terribly. Then life seemed to settle into a different routine. She sent Jacob FAXes and letters, spoke to him on the phone. He came home a few weekends, and Josie was thrilled to be with him. But the time seemed too brief. When he had gone again, she began to think about her art more, started two new paintings, as if trying to recapture her life as it had been before. She read books she had been collecting that Glenda had recommended. A friend from the women's group mentioned a climbing expedition in Alaska and an artists' colony in Italy.

Josie reorganized her apartment, tossing out piles of papers belonging to Bill that she had never done anything about.

There were days, with Jacob gone, that Josie thought she could to on like this, thinking and planning, imagining. You could stay young forever that way, she supposed, or convince yourself you were. Change jobs and friends or move, take a new boyfriend. Josie's mother had told her a few months ago this was no way to live a normal life. There has to be an order to the world, her mother said. She had sent Josie an article from the newspaper: "You Can't Live All Your Lives At Once."

But inside yourself you always feel the same, Josie thought, whether you're fifteen or thirty-five. Some days she felt as she had with Al Minet, no more grownup than that.

You could tell yourself there was time for everything. But maybe one day it wouldn't feel right. It might feel as if you had let something important slip by. Or as if you had been dreaming, Josie realized, dreaming your life away.

Jacob had to go directly to Japan from California. He phoned Josie before he left. "Just another few weeks away. After that, it's the end of traveling, at least for awhile."

"Another few weeks," she said. "I hope it won't be the end of us."

"Travel is part of my job," Jacob replied abruptly. Then his voice softened. "This isn't a way to have a relationship, though. I called work yesterday, told them I had to cut down on travel. You'll come with me next time." He paused. "I miss you more than you could know."

Josie grasped the phone receiver tightly, as if trying to bring him closer.

Jacob phoned once from Japan, but the connection was poor, so Josie sent a FAX to his hotel. Jacob sent one back. Late on Saturday afternoon, she went to the pharmacy to pick up the message. It read:

Coming back early to surprise you! I've been in Japan six days and these are the FAX: God created the world in six days. Then he rested. At home. Will you make a home with me? I love you. WILL YOU MARRY ME? Replay ASAP. Will be in transit soon. Jacob Benner, I.L.U.

He had drawn a wedding ring and two smiling faces.

Josie read the message twice. Her heart pounded wildly. She stared at the word marry, the word love.

The pharmacy was filled with customers. A woman reached in front of Josie now for a bottle of aspirin. Josie looked at the medicines lined on the shelves, a jumble of products—extra-strength, mild, for the unusually sensitive. people were choosing what they wanted, without hesitation, as if there were an order in the world that told one what to do when. For headache you do A, for toothache do B, for long distance marriage proposal you do C.

"Is there something else?" the pharmacist asked her. "Do you need to send a reply? We close in a few minutes."

The pharmacy was closed on Sundays, too. Josie asked for a reply sheet, then copied Jacob's number onto it. For a moment, looking at his quickly scrawled printing "I love you. WILL YOU MARRY ME?" she felt afraid. She wanted to tell Jacob now much she loved him. But maybe she didn't want to be married, like Glenda said. Or maybe she needed more time. But even with all the time in the world, who was going to give her a guarantee?

Josie hesitated, and then it was done, as if she had been holding onto a cliff, dangling and jumped. She wrote in big bold letters: I LOVE YOU. YES. She gave the sheet to the pharmacist and waited as he made the connection.

When she saw the paper disappear into the facsimile machine, it seemed like magic—her message going to Jacob in seconds. She felt suddenly lighter, freer, happy, as if she were soaring in the air, not falling at all.

RONNA WINEBERG BLASER lives in Nashville and is a lawyer by training. Her fiction has appeared in *American Way*, *Colorado Review*, and *Midstream*, and she was the John Atherton Scholar in fiction at the Bread Loaf Writer's Conference.

Patricia S. Boatner

Give Us A Kiss

I stand before the door, key in hand, and I hesitate.

Ten o'clock, Carrie has told me. "We'll meet you at ten o'clock. Oh, and Kate, don't be late. I'm not sure I can go in without you."

I'm not late. I'm never late. I don't want to be here. I want to be on a plane back to the city, back to the comfort of my orderly life. I'm only here, at this house surrounded by smoky blue mountains, because it has to be done and Carrie can't do it without me. And I am not late.

In fact, I'm early. My watch reads nine-thirty. I have come early deliberately to get a head start, to pack away pictures and clean out the dresser — to head off as many crying spells as I can.

I know Carrie will cry. For a week now, Carrie has cried at every call, every card, every condolence wish. And I have paused each time to comfort her and hear her say, "Oh, Kate, I wish I were strong like you."

I don't feel strong. I feel tired. I'm here to keep from making another trip to do this. And I'm early because my sister can't control her emotions.

I turn the key in the rusty lock and open the door. The old house releases a familiar sweet odor — a combination of ancient wood, generations of cooking, smoldering fireplace logs, and musty air that assails my senses. Holding my breath, I push back the curtains and open the living room windows. In the meadow across the small creek, daffodils wave, as they have each spring as long as I can remember. For an instant, I think

66

I must go, as I always did, and gather an armful for the vase on the coffee table. No time, I think, turning. And why bother now? My gaze moves over the familiar room and the pictures on the piano reach out as if they hold life, trying to hold me. I busy myself opening up the rest of the windows, drawing in honeysuckle scent on the spring air to freshen the house.

Such a small house. In the room we once shared, I can reach out and touch my bed and Carrie's with one span of my arms. My dressing room is larger now. Did the room somehow grow in years past to accommodate laughing girls holding slumber parties, trying on prom gowns, dressing for weddings?

Something stirs within the house. The breeze, surely, and yet I'm uneasy. A whisper, somewhere, "Give us a kiss, love."

Be sensible, I tell myself. There is no one here.

But I'm wrong.

"Wherever you go, I go," the whisper says, and I'm a child again.

"How, Momma, how?" the child asks. "You can't go all the way to school with me, can you?"

Momma tucks the blanket in around the child, smiling. "Of course I can. You're part of me and I'm part of you, because you're my little girl. And no matter where you are, if you close your eyes and think of me, I'll be with you." She shakes her head and turns down the lamp. "But I don't think you'll need me, Katie, love. I think you'll take care of yourself very nicely. Now, give us a goodnight kiss."

The child squirms in the embrace and then she's gone. They're both gone, and I sit on the bed alone.

I bolt from the room, half expecting to find someone in the hall. I remember overhearing Momma once, saying to a friend, "Such a strong and sensible girl, my Katie is." Pride filled me then. Now I stand in the hall and wonder why I'm suddenly weak-kneed and insensible.

I will not do this, I tell myself. I'm not here for melancholy memories. There are things to be done, an inventory to take, the house to clean, the estate to settle. And Carrie will be here soon.

I begin with Momma's dresser. I work quickly, making a list, placing objects in a cardboard carton. Makeup, brushes, creams, valueless things. A box with costume jewelry. Momma has given us the good pieces long ago. The diamond from her engagement ring flashes as I lift my right hand.

"I had it reset for you," she tells me on the morning of my sixteenth birthday. "Now, if you like, you can give us a kiss."

The sixteen-year-old likes it so much she give Momma two quick kisses on the cheek.

I drop the jewelry box in the carton and leave the bedroom. I'm on the edge of an unfamiliar precipice and I must find a way back to firm ground before Carrie arrives.

I set up a carton in the living room and start a new list. The Family Bible, careful not to open it. The photograph albums. And the pictures lined up on the piano top. Two girls in caps and gowns, and the same two in white wedding dresses. I meet my own eyes, as dry then as they are now. Carrie cries, Momma cries, everyone cries but the bride.

"Stop making a spectacle of yourself," the bride tells her sister.

"Spectacle!" Carrie wipes her cheeks. "I don't understand you. Everybody cries at a wedding."

"Katie has better self-control than you or me," Momma says. "Ah, if only your Poppa could have lived to see the two of you grow up. He'd be so proud. Just as I am. Come here, my girls, and give us a kiss before we go into the church."

"Careful of the headpiece," the bride says, and offers a cheek.

The bride's photo goes into the carton face down and I can't breathe. I step to the window and fill my lungs with fresh air. Then I see the African violet. The earth around the roots is cracked and dried, the leaves wilted and thirsty for attention, for the tender touch of her hands. The pot still wears the wide red ribbon as it sits on the sill where she had me put it the last time I was here, so many months ago.

"I hope you like it," I tell her. "I know African violets are your favorite things in the world."

"Well, maybe not my very favorite," she says, her smile cutting deep furrows into her face. "But they are close behind my girls." She reaches up and I lean down to kiss her forehead.

I turn from the window, frantically seeking a safe spot. I find myself facing the portrait over the mantel. The young woman in it has smooth skin and a warm smile, and the same straight nose I recognize in my own reflection. Beside her is the man I never knew, and each of them holds a dark-haired girl. Once child snuggles against her shoulder. The other sits rigidly on his knee.

I grip the mantel as tightly as I'd gripped the phone last week. "I just wanted to hear your voice," Momma says, and her words are so low I think we must have a bad connection.

"Are you sure you're better?" I ask.

"I'm fine, Katie love. I think I'll be going home tomorrow."

I'm relieved. "Momma, I'm really sorry I couldn't get in while you were in the hospital."

"Nonsense. You've called almost every day, and there's been nothing to do here."

"I love you, Momma. And I'll get home soon, I promise."

"I know, Katie. I love you too, and I do wish you were here to give us a kiss."

I'm never late. I arrive in time to make all the arrangements, greet all the callers, organize all the business matters.

My knuckles are white from gripping the mantel. The fireplace beneath it yawns dark and empty, with no warmth radiating from the banked ash, and I turn, shaking and cold.

Carrie is here. She is coming up the walk, two strong young men behind her carrying more cartons for packing.

I cannot stay. I have stepped over the precipice and I'm

falling. I must find a refuge, find my strength again.

"Kate. Oh, good, I'm so glad you're already here."

"No," I say.

"What?" Carrie stares at me. They all stare at me.

"No." Inside I have screamed, but the voice I hear is faint. "Not today. I can't today. Maybe tomorrow. I don't know when, but not today." The tears I never cry come now, too fast, and I can't say more.

"Oh, Kate!" Carrie's eyes fill, too, and she reaches for me, because I'm strong. But I step away from her, because I'm sensible. And my sensibility tells me I need all my strength for myself this time.

I stumble to the door and as I step outside into the shadow of the mountain, I hear the whisper again from somewhere inside. "Give us a kiss, Katie love."

A sense of urgency propels me, tells me I mustn't stop or I'm lost, and yet — how can I be more lost than now? I lift my gaze to the mountaintops, where the glare of the morning sun has burned off the haze, and I hesitate — just long enough to look once more toward home, raise trembling fingers to my lips, and toss a kiss back over the threshold.

PATRICIA S. BOATNER is a Mississippi native, transplanted in the early 1970s to her east Tennessee home of Lenoir City. Her writing career includes several years as a newspaper writer/ editor, a novel entitled *All Our Tomorrows*, and a one-act play featured in the anthology, *Mississippi Writers:Reflections of Childhood and Youth, Vol. 4: Drama*.

Bill Brown

Flashed

My grandfather flashed
the tops of fence posts,
hammering galvanized steel.
With bodock, a song
and a prayer, or nails
snapped beyond repair.
A wood like him,
beautifully grained
and knotted inside
but too hard to crack.

He rode his horse through
the pastures addressing
his cows by name, heifers
that started with Ms:
Matilda, Martha, Maggie,
Mary, May...
They stopped grazing
and followed him single-file
around the farm, some for hay,
some just to see what
the old man was up to.

Thirty years later,
GrandMilt long dead,
I detour off the interstate
between Memphis and Nashville
and drive to Bible Hills.
I don't see any ghost
in the cemetery, but the old
house is still lived in,
the lake behind the barn

grown up in willows.
The three hundred acres
sold and divided by five.

A new tractor kicks
a line of dust in a corn field,
and a boy is combing a horse
through the open door
of the barn.
A few fence posts flashed
by my grandfather still stand,
rotting from the ground up,
but the metal, a modeled pewter,
still mirrors the sun.

How We Spent Our Summer Vacation, 1956

At the beginning of each
school year when kids
stood in front of class
and announced that they
had been to Disneyland
or Myrtle Beach,
my sister and I sat tight-lipped.

What could we say:
that we had visited our grandparents
on the Tennessee River
three counties away,
learned to string barbed wire,
talk to cows, run from billy goats,
watch for rattlesnakes,
sleep in a dog-trot on a feather mattress,
fish tight-lined for eels in Cub Creek,
spy ghosts haunting the Primitive
Baptist Cemetery, hurtle the rat snake
in the corn crib, feed rotten tomatoes
to chickens, and every night
before listening to an old stand-up
radio, hear a stern-faced little man
with gentle hands, say the only three
sentences he had said all day
in a prayer blessing supper?

After the dishes were dried
and *The Shadow* had exacted
his special justice, my sister and I
sat up as my grandparents slept
and watched a family of skunks
dance in moonlight across the road.
What could we say?

Laundry

No hidden grief could survive
my mother's kitchen table;
strangers and neighbors
paraded through our house.
The young Baptist minister,
too kind for the politics
of a small town church;
the family doctor who loved
his nurse, his brother's wife;
the Korean bride who followed
her GI husband home
to become his family's maid;
the garbage man whose professor son
wouldn't acknowledge his father.
Most days the confessional opened
and our cereal and milk
sat on the front porch bannister.
My sister and I imagined their stories:
The spinster aunt who had forced her
nephew to drink lye; the impotent football star
whose fiancee felt was so honorable and shy;
The farmer who was too affectionate
with his Shetland pony;
The Hawthornean holy man
whose soul was as black as satan's.
Our mother knew them all.
Her understanding smile could coax
a tight rosebud to blossom, a clenched fist
to unfold the lifeline of its palm.
Maybe this explains my family's
active dream-world. We learned early to lock
our sorrows deep inside. As the kitchen door
closed and visitors kept the back door open,
our closets began to swell. At night

they inflated like lifeboats, bulged like
early plums before rust blighted the harvest.
How lucky we were, our neighbors thought,
as they watched our laundry bright
behind the kitchen window,
billowing and twisting
in our secret storm.

BILL BROWN is a native of west Tennessee, with three published collections of poetry: *Holding On by Letting Go*, *What the Night Told Me*, and *The Art of Dying*. He currently lives in Greenbrier.

Katherine Bryant

Songs from the Fifth Grade

It was a lesson too late (soon) for the (my) learning. This I know. Now this I know. . .

School began on a steamy Tennessee August day in an inner-city elementary school. But this time, instead of being a student, I was the teacher. Fresh from graduate school, my diploma and teaching credentials still warm, I charged into the world of chalk dust and summer-fed students. There was no air conditioning, few supplies, and thirty-five sweating bodies constantly asking to go to the bathroom or the water fountain. I was afraid to show them how to make paper fans for fear they'd turn into UFOs and I'd lose what little control I actually had in the room. I was trying to concentrate on long division and basal readers rather than the slow buzzing of summer insects outside the open windows or the smells of turnip greens cooking in the cafeteria near my room. We were all distracted.

Fifth grade center was Bobby McEwen. I was somewhere on the sidelines in that room even if I was supposed to be in front as the captain of this team of ten-year-olds. The jumping and singing young man in the third row at the back had our complete attention. Bobby was the star player on the asphalt courts beyond where I parked my car and he also held court in all the classrooms he'd graced so far in his brief life. I didn't fool myself, I knew I wasn't even in the game even if I did have the ruler and the big desk. Meanwhile, I marked in white chalk the figures of ten divided by two (which was supposed to be five) and prayed that this horrible child would eventually take his place, hopefully before the patrolling principal walked by.

Bobby McEwen hopped from foot to foot, pointing out much more interesting facts about what was really going on in the white clapboard house across the street from school. He sang:

"Hey, what's goin' on, Mrs. Jones. We got a THANG goin' on. . ."

The answer to the real problem posed that morning was never ten—unless it was the ten men queued on the porch at Mrs. Jones' establishment. Some of them sat in the rusted motel chairs to avoid the hot wind. Others just smoked and talked, waiting their turns. Various men from various walks of life were certainly multiplying, but that wasn't the math I was trying to teach in the fifth grade. And even twenty-three year old me could deduce that there were more than platonic visitations happening at Mrs. Jones' house. Since Bobby and most of the other children actually knew most of those visitors and called them by name, I had no chance of teaching anything even remotely as important or interesting as the who's who from that porch. Mrs. Verna Jones, prostitute, was teaching, and Mr. Bobby McEwen, wiseguy student, was teaching. I was just the unfortunate person pretending to be the teacher.

Relief came when I heard Bobby's sneakers squeaking out the classroom door. I chalked along happily relieved, hoping then that the fifth grade might look at me more favorably now that the class hoodlum had cleared out. However, it was then that the principal, whom we all called Madame X behind her back, chose to begin stalking the halls with a paddle in her right hand, gently but ominously tapping her left palm. SHE searched and destroyed her prey, her large lanky form moving like a big cat. SHE caught Bobby just as he was tearing towards the back door exit aimed out of the building and into his favorite hideout—the bushes under the kindergarten room. He liked to play hide-and-seek beneath the safety of the barbarous holly bushes. He liked to make noises to scare the five-year-olds above him. God knows what other things he did in there, but even I felt sorry for him when he was captured by Madame X. I didn't know then that these two creatures understood each other in a way I'd never be able to mimic.

"Miss Bryant," Madame X bellowed, "I have found this fellow about to leave the building. Isn't he supposed to be in YOUR room?" I looked sheepishly at her because the paddle moved ominously up and down in the rhythm of her speech and I wasn't sure who was about to get it, Bobby or me.

I replaced the chalk neatly in the tray at the base of the blackboard and replied,"Yes, Mr. McEwen was about to go to my car for something I'd left there."

Both Bobby and Madame X looked at me incredulously. SHE turned suspiciously, but he was curious about my sudden defense. I stood—chalkless, paddleless, and defenseless—before the two most powerful people in the fifth grade and an audience of giggly children. I had no inkling or thought of what to do when my voice sent itself into the warm sir.

"Thank you, Bobby, that is my special pencil, the one I asked you for." I said, quickly extracting the red pencil with my name on it from behind his left ear. he'd obviously stolen it from my desk earlier. At last my years of not being a perfect child myself had come in handy. During the precariousness of my own childhood in West Tennessee and adolescence in the North, I'd learned to think quickly and to invent realities as they suited my situation.

Madame X sniffed and left quietly with, "Perhaps, Miss Bryant, you might choose a more reliable student than our friend bobby here for your errands. He has a tendency to get LOST between here and the parking lot."

After that incident, I had captured Bobby's imagination. It turned out that the pivotal point at which we began to teach each other. We made a deal that he'd stand near the front of the room during match so that most of the students would either look at him or me during the observations of passing principals or visiting fathers over at the Jones place. He named himself my bodyguard. He taught me some of his songs and I taught him mine. We rode together in my ragtop beetle as the weather deepened and the holly bushes made their red berries. We were quiet about our alliance so neither of us would get in trouble with our peers for fraternizing with the enemy.

But the day came in February when I took a few days leave for a course at the teacher center called "Disciplinary Techniques for Young Children." And that was also the day Bobby went AWOL from school again. I had called my sub at lunch to explain the next day's lesson and asked him about attendance. It seems Bobby never came back from his lunch period. So I feigned a headache and left my small group of young teachers discussing positive discipline techniques and went after Bobby to head him off before SHE found him and he again felt the sting from her paddle as she extended her philosophy, "You have to hit these children so they know you love them. That's what they're used to. And it is what works here."

"Bobby McEwen, I know you're in those bushes. Now come out right now before SHE comes after you," I pleaded to the silent shrubbery.

I waited for some minutes, the rough grass staining the wool pants my mother had given me for Christmas. I was sure I heard his breathing and hoped it wasn't some rodent or dog rather than Bobby. Finally patience and paranoia (about being seen by anyone) waned and I moved in for the kill. Skirting along the brick wall, feeling for flesh and bone, and bleeding from the holly pricks, I crept into Bobby's territory. When I found a soft earthy spot I eased down, silently lamenting my ruined pants. I waited for my eyes to adjust. I knew he was there because he was humming and moving as usual, and I recognized Diana Ross' latest tune. I prepared to wait for minutes, weeks, years — or until SHE found us both. I was practicing positive discipline. It was cold, so to keep my mind alert, I thought about the day in October when Bobby had taken me to the housing project where he lived. He'd had me stop nearing a burning dumpster where several scary-looking characters were smoking cigarettes or something and passing a brown paper bag among them. I told him I'd wait until I saw him safely into his house and he'd given me a puzzled look. My mother's protocol—to always see my friends to their doors—was obviously out of place in this environment. But we do live by our own patterns. Bobby swaggered toward the men and spoke to them, then waved to me before disappearing behind a screenless door into a life unknown to me. I'd understood who was protecting whom as my car eased past the smoking dumpster and out of the area with no words or dangers befalling me. I smiled.

"Miss Bryant."

"Yes."

"You, there?"

"Yes, Bobby."

"SHE had to go to some meeting and you was gone, so I figured I'd better get outa that room before I had to do something to that man. Wanna go down to the store and get a Milky Way?

"Sure."

Bobby held my hand to guide me through the brambles to safety. As was often true, Bobby knew everything that was really important to know his city. I knew that I was putting a student into my car in full view of several classrooms and I didn't have parental permission to take this student for a ride and I was AWOL from my own class at the teacher center. But I had learned well from Bobby that year. The moral here was: One does not stay in an environment one does not understand nor have some control over. By our wits and cooperation we were both passing the fifth grade so far.

We spent that afternoon together. He gave me a tour of the neighborhood and I learned many of the actual reasons why some of my students seemed distracted much of the time. Bobby gave me life stories and interconnections that were important to know when trying to get things done in that elementary school population. Late that afternoon it started to snow. I dropped him off near that same rusted dumpster by his home which he would still absolutely not let me enter. I watched his small brave frame move like a plastic figure in a plastic shaker paperweight from Disneyland or Miami Beach. And I understood why Bobby could never stand still and why he sang most of the time. His was a sad and desperate setting framed in poverty and neglect, but he had taught himself to cope using his music, movement, and bravado. His inner world moved him along the dangerous passages of the external one. He was a leader in basketball and a leader of the pack in the fifth grade, but I suspected horrors behind the doors I saw him disappear behind that evening.

I'd like to say that after our encounters, Bobby McEwen became a brilliant model student and I became an exemplary young teacher, and that we both lived happily ever after. But the truth is that Madame X wrote me a fine recommendation praising me as a good teacher and the following year I got a "better" job in a junior high school in a "better" school. Bobby was passed to the sixth grade but never attended the middle school he was zoned for. By then, thanks to Bobby's tips, I'd learned to teach more than just what was found in textbooks. I'd learned that the environs of any place, but particularly a classroom, extends to the landscapes of the neighborhood and way beyond the walls that try to hold its inhabitants. The sights, sounds, smells, and touches of anyplace form and provide context for the people who live there and that is where one begins teaching others. The methodologies Bobby had taught me would probably last longer than the multiplication table I'd taught him. Frankly, after our year in the fifth grade, our loss of contact, I didn't drive to his apartment or try hard to find him. Our time together was over, but I still treasured that young boy and think of him often in the twenty years since. The end of our story is the end of a folk song I used to favor:

Are you goin' away with no words of farewell
Will there be not a trace left behind?

Bobby and I left traces on each other. We'd both learned and taught, but I more than he. I like to think that I taught him that all adults, especially teachers, weren't bad and that his street savvy was another way of knowing we're valuable. I'd learned that teaching is perhaps the best way to learn. Perhaps our traces were invisible; but now, if I close my eyes, I can see us in that Volkswagen, rolling down hot black pavements in the "bad" part of town, smelling the acrid burning of a dumpster, feeling moist earth outside the kindergarten room, and tasting soft Milky Ways and icy cokes from the store on the corner across from the Jones house. We'd learned the sounds of each other's songs.

KATHERINE BRYANT has a background in journalism, technical writing, and is currently Director of Writing Across the Curriculum at Tennessee State University. She lives in Nashville.

Anne Hall Dougherty

Changing Curtains

Before breakfast was ready on Monday, Granny called three times to update me on the cold that had been creeping up on her like spring mud over the weekend and now was full blown. "I think I'm ill," she told me with the first call. The second time, her voice lowered a few levels, and she whispered, "My fever is raging." With this last call, I started to worry a little. I know Mama says Granny can draw illnesses out of a hat like a magician when it suits her purposes, but, still, she's old. By the time the telephone rang the third time, Mama was slamming pots and pans in the kitchen, and I almost jumped out of my skin when the bell jangled.

"Attention grabbing old woman," Mama scoffed, leaning around the corner into the hallway where the phone hung in a small alcove. Her head disappeared as I grabbed the receiver.

"Granny?"

"Jane, I'm dying. Tell your mama not to worry about the curtains, though." Her voice sounded weak, but brave.

"Granny, I promise, I'll be over after breakfast. Don't fret," I pleaded. Behind me, I heard Mama slam a plate on the dining room table and stomp back into the kitchen. "My breakfast's ready, and I'll be right over as soon as I'm done." All I heard was raspy breathing at her end. I couldn't stand it, so I rushed on, "You know Mama won't let me come until I eat." The air in the alcove was stuffy, and I wiped the sweat from my forehead. Granny finally said with a drawn out sigh, "I suppose that will do." I laid the receiver down. For a minute, I was tempted to leave it off the hook, but, if I did, I figured my grandmother would just call Pete Sanders, our sheriff, to drive all the way out here to hang up the phone.

When I entered the dining room, I caught Mama with her ear to the hallway door. "Her temperature's up," I said.

She dusted the doorknob vigorously. "Well, fine, I hope it burns some of the stubbornness from her," Mama said. Her dark eyes snapped. "But I won't help her hang the curtains. It's a useless chore, and both of us are too old to go around climbing on ladders." With a snort, she returned to the kitchen, kicking the swinging door closed with one foot.

Sighing, I sat down at the table and stared at the greasy eggs in front of me. All I ever wanted for breakfast was toast and jam, and all I ever got was eggs dripping with bacon grease. Well, I didn't like them, but my grandmother did. "Maybe I should take a plate to Granny," I yelled at the closed door. I heard a muffled "Humph!" and was satisfied; I really hadn't expected Mama to answer at all.

There was no way that grease was going to get past the knot in my stomach, and I shoved the plate away. From the window, a warm breeze drifted into the dining room and ruffled the edges of the lace tablecloth. The late September morning floated light and clear around the yard, but on the mountain peaks that peered over the maples at the edge of the lawn, the air was already cold. The thought of autumn waiting in the mountains made me guilty, and I fingered the brochures from Maryville College that my mother placed by my plate each morning to remind me that I was supposed to be there. Classes started last week, and Daddy had already written the tuition check, smiling at me. "You're ready to make your own way," he told me, but I raced from the room, praying my tears would hold until I reached the safety of my room. Daddy hadn't said anything more about leaving, and I lingered on in the house, sitting passively amid the rapidly changing seasons.

How could I tell my parents I couldn't leave? I was the peacemaker in the family, the calm in the center of my mother's and grandmother's lifelong tornado. Ever since I could remember, they have fussed and fumed at one another like two boiling tea kettles on opposite sides of the stove. If I left, I was afraid they would just wear themselves out with all that arguing and float over the mountains, sputtering like two balloons with the air seeping out. And it would be my fault.

Just look at what they were doing now. Every year on the first on October, Granny removed the flimsy lace curtains of summer and replaced them with floor length drapes of weighty green brocade edged with satin roses, her winter drapes. I helped her drag the musty smelling curtains from the cedar closet to the back yard where we beat them with a wicker racquet until the dust flew everywhere. Then we dragged the awkward drapes inside, but only my grandmother hung them, since this was her ritual, not mine. I sat cross-legged on the floor and caught the summer curtains as she shook them down to me like cobwebs. Once the winter drapes were hung, the house assumed a somber air befitting our harsh mountain winters, and my grandmother was satisfied. But as she grew older, Granny could no long maneuver the heavy material over the windows. I tried to help, but I was too short to reach the hooks. Then, Daddy hung the curtains, but then his arthritis got so bad, we knew his curtain hanging days were over. Mama thinks changing curtains to suit the seasons is just inventing work so she has always refused to help. So there we were, and here I stay.

Yesterday, I called Maryville College and said I was sick, borrowing Granny's illness for a little while like a blouse or a hat. It wasn't serious, I said, just a summer cold that forgot the change of seasons. Good news, I told my parents that night at supper, classes don't start for another week, after the first of October. They looked at me, then each other. Daddy closed his eyes and shook his head, and Mama let it go, her arms crossed and lips pursed tightly.

Today, I didn't want to think about either curtains or leaving. Instead, I pushed back my chair and carried my plate into the kitchen. Mama didn't speak, but when she moved away from the counter, I saw a plate ready for Granny, all done up in a basket with a damp dish towel over the top to keep it warm. Thank goodness, I sighed. It's easier to coax a bone from a dog than it is to persuade Mama to do something she doesn't want to do. I started to thank her, but she waved me away like a worrisome fly. When I reached the back door, though, she said, "I suppose I can carry her to the doctor if you think its necessary." I sighed again. To my mother's scorn, Granny was skittish about doctors and insisted upon medicating herself with pungent smelling home remedies she picked from her herb garden and brewed for days on the back of the stove. She drank the concoctions straight from Mason jars like most of us drink water. But it was an old argument between them, much older than this summer cold, so I waved my hand dismissing the suggestion. Mama nodded. "But," she added, "tell her I won't change the curtains for her even if tomorrow is the first of October."

I groaned and headed down the steps. I guess I was going to think about curtains whether I wanted to or not. Now, Granny might say Mama is acting out of spite in refusing to help. But Mama truly sees the curtain changing as an unnecessary effort. Curtains are curtains, she always said. She is a woman of few wasted steps, and the steps she takes are always crisp and brisk. Granny, on the other hand, is more a woman of rhythms and tides. No calendar is ever needed to prompt Granny to exchange her summer ginghams for winter wool. Airy doilies are whisked from the back and chairs and underneath lamps and replaced by rose-colored, straw mats as soon as the sun is low enough in the early evening to hit her eyes from the kitchen window as she prepares her supper. Pansies in spring, coreopsis and black-eyed susans in summer, asters and mums in fall — such is Granny's alliance with the seasons, and just as surely as nature changed the seasons, so did my grandmother change her curtains.

Maybe the difference between the two lay not so much in genes as surroundings. Mama was raised in town where time is measured by clocks and whistles. Granny, though, was born on Eagle's Bald, a little pinpoint of grass lying gracefully across the mountain top like starched linen thrown carelessly over a table. There wasn't much company on the isolated farm other than a few cows and the rustling of the constant wind through the firs and oaks. When you live this close to the mountain, the human way of doing things gets kind of lost in nature's way of doing things. Oh, yes, if Granny's cold kept her trapped in bed tomorrow, winter would still show up, but, without changing her curtains, my grandmother would be miserably out of step with her world.

Quickly, I ran across the yard to Granny's house next door, the basket of food knocking awkwardly against my hip. Her house sat hidden behind a row of maples, standing like soldiers on the boundary line between the two properties. Much of my childhood was spent playing here between the tree branches, one foot diplomatically in each yard, so that even if Mama and Granny couldn't see into each other's kitchen, they could see me.

As I broke through the trees, I saw the slight flutter of the summer curtain in Granny's room. She was waiting for me. I hurried up the curved staircase and crossed the dark hallway, my hand sweating beneath the still warm plate. When I reached her room, Granny was back in bed, the quilt drawn tightly to her neck. Her heavy, square jaw with its jutting chin rose from the quilt like the prow of a battle ship, and I smiled as I crossed the bare wooden floor. Actually, I am fond of both Mama and Granny equally, though this seems to displease them equally, too, since I never took sides. Of course, Granny said my failure to take sides showed a distinct lack of backbone, like Daddy. I silently resented this observation, but Daddy only smiled. Anybody who can survive eighteen years of bickering Lowrys with their senses intact, he told me, surely has more than her fair share of backbone. It was good, I often thought, that the relationship between Mama and Granny only seemed to amuse Daddy; the battles of the women might wear a man with less humor clean away.

Granny didn't move as I crossed the room, but she was only playing possum. I knew because I could see her blue eyelids twitching in the morning sun. I pulled the rocker up close to the bed and sat down, laying the warm basket on the bedside table. I figured the smell, if nothing else, would cause Granny to acknowledge me, but I was wrong. The cold's interruption of her plans was really worrying her. Whenever something irritated my grandmother, she just became real still and silent like a slow smoldering fire until she got her way out of sheer stubbornness.

As the minutes passed, I began to get restless. Usually, I avoided quiet times that invited reflections since I have so much on my mind lately. So, I reached out and tapped Granny's gnarled hand gently, but she didn't respond. Well, I could wait, too. One thing you learn being on the tail end of Granny's comet is patience. From the foothills at the edge of town came the low rumble of the morning train as it edged its way around the mountains. I ought to be on that train, I thought again, and the solitary horn blast was reproachful. As always, the window panes vibrated slightly with the passing rail cars, and, at first, I thought Granny's bed was also trembling from the train's roar. When I looked again, I saw instead that she was shivering, deep, rolling shudders that rocked the bed like a cradle.

Alarmed, I jumped up and placed my hand against her forehead. The skin felt dry and hot, yet she continued her possum act. But there are just some times it is best not to cater to Granny, and I rushed to the bathroom for a damp cloth to soak some of the heat from her skin. As I hurried down the hall, a voice inside me said *it's for sure you can't leave now.*

"Jane," Granny whispered when I returned with the washcloth. As I laid the cloth across her forehead, I grasped one of her hands in mine. I knew she disliked such signs of affection, but she was too weak to pull her hand back. The sun had inched its way over the window sill and now rolled across the bed like a floodlight at the foot of a stage. Grandmother laid with her chin turned upward as if tanning herself. In the harsh sunlight, the lines of her face drooped like melting ice until it seemed as if only her strong jaw was holding her features up.

"The curtains are worrying me something dreadful." she said. She plucked fretfully at the loose strings of the guilt around her chest, and her eyes filled with tears. When she turned her head to me, though, I saw she wasn't sad, but angry, and I pulled back slightly. Even infirm, Granny's anger is nothing to laugh at. "Tomorrow is October 1. I have to change the curtains tomorrow," she insisted. She struggled to rise, and I held her down. Angrily, she swatted at my arms over and over, but most of the weak blows missed. With a wheezing cough, she fell back on the bed, defeated, and I felt cold. I rarely saw Granny defeated. Like an insult, the summer curtains billowed gracefully in the breeze.

I was still standing uncertainly by the bed when Mama wandered into the room, looking surprised, like she hadn't expected my grandmother and me to be there. She said casually, "I've come to fetch the plate." Beneath her mound of covers, Granny attempted a snort, but ended up coughing instead. As the hacking sounds filled the room, Mama finally looked at Granny, and her eyes narrowed until they were black slits. Then she frowned at the ceiling.

"Well," Mama said as she mulled over Granny's real life illness, one hand worrying with the strings of her spotless apron. The two of them glared at each other over the bed as we all silently contemplated this dilemma. I could see Mama was worried, despite herself. "Maybe we should call Dr. Jenkins after all," she told me. Granny shook her head back and forth on the pillow, and Mama looked back down at her. "If we're going to get the curtains up in time," she added.

I looked at her, surprised, but Mama's face was still, so I glanced at Granny instead, my neck growing tense from the unspoken argument taking place over my head. Granny scowled. There was no way for Granny to win this one if she wanted her curtains hung, but she made us wait. Mama never moved, but my feet shifted uneasily until Mama placed a hand on my arm. Then, Granny nodded once, and Mama nodded back. Weakly, Granny fumbled for her water jar on the bed-side table, but her hand fell a few inches short. Reaching around me for the jar, Mama sloshed some water in a glass. Gently, she brought the glass to my grandmother's parched lips, her strong arm behind the old woman's frail shoulders.

"Fine," said Mama briskly, "we'll call Dr. Jenkins. While he's here, I guess I might as well drag those old drapes out of the cedar closet."

"You know," Granny said as a few drops of water trick-led indelicately down the creases in her cheeks and off the end of the famous jaw, "I'm feeling a little hungry."

Later, I sat outside in the sun on the front stoop, out of the way. A dogwood leaf, the color of dried blood, fluttered down to rest between my feet. Daddy wandered over from our yard and picked it up, and, with a smile, handed it to me like a bouquet. I looked back at the old house I thought so grand and saw Mama's shadow stretching in front of the window, a sum-mer curtain hung around her neck. Just behind her, a smaller shadow, my grandmother, sat in a armchair, a quilt around her shoulders and a finger pointed toward the ceiling. I smiled back at Daddy as he wiped the sweat from his face. "Train will be through here in the morning as usual," he said.

"Yes," I said. "I know."

ANNE HALL DOUGHERTY grew up in Nashville and Tullahoma, respectively. She currently resides in Virginia, but confesses continu-al longing for the mountains of east Tennessee.

Thomas M. Edwards

The Corporation Blue Suit

It's been a long time since I wore that suit; a wool, navy blue with vest. And there are other suits and assorted clothing that have not been worn for some time. Every time I enter the walk-in closet, I see those old unused garments. Many times, they have to be pushed aside to get at the clothes I want to wear for the day.

Since retiring to Tennessee, my wardrobe has changed drastically. No more dress suits, white shirts, ties and winged-tip shoes. Oh, there might be an occasional dinner dance or meeting or play that requires dressing up, and maybe a funeral or a rare wedding — but not too often.

The everyday dress is casual; sport shirts, gold shirts, jeans, slacks, monogrammed golf cap, cotton socks, tennis shoes and even shorts. But never a navy blue, wool suit with vest and the two- and three-piece business suits with shirts and neckwear.

My wife has frequently mentioned that her share of closet space is less than equitable and if I don't remedy this overcrowded situation, she will take matters into her own hands.

These distinguished suits must be moved elsewhere. The question is where can they be stored and preserved so they won't be in the way? Our attic is packed with relics and prized mementos of the glorious days of a bygone work world. The garage is filled with vehicles, garden supplies, tools, paint and hundreds of items that will surely be needed someday. Our home is a virtual treasure chest of memorabilia.

On the other hand, suppose my former company would call me to consult and assist on a major project? Then, I will need this business wardrobe. Of course, they haven't called me in years. Impossible as it sounds, somehow they are operating without me. If that remains true, perhaps I may never, ever need this finery.

But what does one do with an old business wardrobe? What does one do with the sartorial armament of the professional world? How should one treat the prized raiment that guarded you through the marble hallways and oak-paneled board rooms?

Who better to ask than former businessmen in our Tennessee retirement community, who must have faced this same awesome question.

Their answers varied from a complete lack of understanding, to showing absolutely no interest; telling me to give them away, let my spouse throw them out, or donate them to a rummage sale, and even the ungodly mention of their use in washing and polishing my car.

A rummage sale! No! No! My cherished suits deserve a far greater destiny than being merely discarded. And never the navy blue, wool suit with vest. That suit is special. It is my CORPORATION BLUE SUIT.

One of my neighbors did mention a thrift shop in Crossville that accepts clean, used clothing for resale at a nominal charge, with the proceeds going to charity. That sounded good. A deserving charity reaping the benefits from my valued clothes.

The next day I went to the thrift shop located in the center of our small town of Crossville. Upon entering I saw rows and rows of plain brown pipe racks filled with clothing of every description; work pants, jeans, an unusual array of flashy colored leisure suits, old faded polyester slacks, long outdated dress pants; some straight legged, some flared and a few tapered. Shelves were filled with shirts, sweaters, caps, work jackets and socks; the floors lined with an assortment of shoes and boxes of unsorted clothes.

Several people were looking through clothing on the racks and you could hear the scratching sound of hangers against the metal pipes.

I could not find a single suit of the caliber or quality of mine, which would indicate they should be in high demand and sell quickly. This shop will certainly profit from my donation.

A neatly dressed elderly woman was behind the counter.

"Good morning!" I exclaimed.

"Good morning," she replied cheerfully. Then, noticing my armful of clothes, "Just put those on the counter and I'll take care of them."

"Well, before I do, let me tell you about these suits," I said, holding them up. "They've been cleaned and pressed and placed on hangers."

"That's fine," she said. "I'll put them away,"

"These were my regular business suits, but this," I stated, placing the blue suit gently on the counter, "this one is special."

She leaned over the counter and replied, "It looks just like the other ones to me."

"No, this one is special. It's my CORPORATION BLUE SUIT."

"Your what?"

"Let me explain. I worked for a car division of a major automotive corporation. Whenever we were planning or considering major policy changes, financial expenditures, procedural changes, future advertising campaigns, pricing changes or any major planning; we presented our ideas and plans to top members of the corporation for their review, consideration and possible approval. Early in my career, I was wisely advised to wear a conservative, preferably dark blue, business suit to these high-level meetings. A power suit, if you will. It became known as the CORPORATION BLUE SUIT, or just the Corporation Suit."

"Oh, that's nice."

I continued on, "And every time we attended a corporation meeting, and especially if we were making a presentation, we were reminded to wear our Corporation Suit. That's how this particular suit got its name. I thought you might want to know the history before putting it up for sale."

She looked puzzled, "There's really not a big demand here in Crossville for corporation suits."

"And there's more; this suit has witnessed some of the biggest transactions and deals the world has ever known. And the greatest power struggles imaginable. It has been through backbiting and backstabbing, it has seen accolades bestowed on great leaders, the crowning of champions, the humbling of mighty heroes, the depths of despair and the heartbreak of failures. You can say this suit has literally been through blood, sweat and tears."

"Is there something wrong with it?" she asked, handing the suit back to me.

"Oh, no. I just want you to know the background of this suit. For me, it has a lot of memories; some good, some bad."

"Do you want it back?"

"No, I don't have a use for it anymore," I said, handing it back to her.

"This is not an ordinary suit. It's very special. It's not just for anyone."

She slowly took the suit from me. "I'll be sure that a deserving man will get this."

"Thank you, I appreciate that."

I left the thrift shop feeling a great surge of satisfaction, knowing I was helping my fellow man by providing the warmth and strength of my suit.

That night, I had difficulty falling asleep. I couldn't get my mind off that suit. I thought of the many meetings where I wore it, and the favorable outcome of those meetings. Would there be important meetings and conferences in the future where I would benefit by wearing that suit? Did I do the right thing in disposing of it?

The next morning I discussed the problem with my wife.

"I keep thinking of my Corporation Suit," I said, "and whether I should have held onto it."

She looked at me rather thoughtfully and replied, "I know you're concerned. That is a very nice-looking suit, and perhaps it wouldn't hurt to have it around. You never know when there might be a really special occasion to wear it."

"It's too late," I said dejectedly. "I'm sure by now someone bought it."

"Well, maybe not. They've only had it for a day."

"That was my favorite," I replied sadly. I don't know if we would be here today if it wasn't for that suit."

"I know," she replied understandingly. "I didn't realize how much that suit meant to you. Why don't you go back to the shop and see if it might still be there."

Within minutes I was on my way to Crossville, not knowing what to expect. I hoped that in spite of being an outstanding value, my favorite suit would be there.

I rushed into the store and began looking through the racks.

"Good morning," said the same lady who had taken my clothes the previous day.

"Good morning," I said eagerly. "I don't know if you remember me. I was in here yesterday and donated some business suits."

"I remember, you're the one with that. . .what did you call it, Corporation Blue Suit?"

"Yes, that's it! If it's still here I'd like to take it back."

"Oh," she said. "It was sold right after you left."

"It was? Oh, dear, oh my gosh."

I slowly walked to the door. "Do you suppose I might inquire how much it sold for?"

Her eyes lit up. "Ten dollars! We got ten dollars for it."

Ten dollars, I thought. My priceless suit went for ten dollars. That's not right.

"You might like to know," she continued, "The new

young minister from the local mission church bought it."

A new minister from a mission church bought my COR-PORATION BLUE SUIT. I could hardly believe my ears.

"Did you say a new minister?" I asked.

"Yes, a nice young man; said he was just out of school and needed a dark suit and yours was perfect. The church is right up the street if you want to talk to him."

"No, I don't need to talk to him. I feel so much better knowing that someone like that new minister has my suit."

"What do you mean?" she asked.

"In his line of work, he will have dragons and demons to fight, insurmountable obstacles to overcome, great power struggles between good and bad, backstabbing and backbiting, humbling experiences, the scorn and resentment of the enemy, thousands of temptations, and the wrath and fury of righteousness. He must be the defender of the faith. A champion. A protector."

"But what does that have to do with your suit?"

I smiled at her and said, "My CORPORATION BLUE SUIT will protect him. It will be his safeguard, his armament and shield. It will do for him what it did for me."

I started walking to the door. "Thank you for sharing that information with me."

"You're very welcome," she said. Then pointing to a clothes rack, she added, "You know, your other old suits didn't sell and are still here. If you want them back, I'll be glad to get them."

I rushed out and quickly closed the door.

Thomas M. Edwards is retired, and now resides in Fairfield Glade, near Crossville. He has written recently on the subject of golf, which occupies much of his time in retirement.

David K. Fenner

Bright Lights

Jeb awakened every morning at five A.M. and today was no different. The world in the trailer was black except for the luminous glow of the clock.

The glow mesmerized him for a short time and he thought of all the watch makers who had died early this century, poisoned by the radium used to coat the watch dials. He wondered why he always had such strange thoughts, not being able sometimes to cast them from his mind for days at a time. As he turned over to touch his wife, a spasm of cough seized him and forced him to sit up. He lit a cigarette to relax his lungs, and ironically, it worked. With each deliberate inhalation and equally slow exhalation he began to arouse, while at the same time becoming calm.

Darkness was such a part of his life. He dreamed in shades of black and gray. His walls were black and irregular during the day, black and flat at night. At home he breathed in untainted air and exhaled misty black air. At work, the air exchange both ways was black.

The burning cigarette seemed to cast as much light as the headlamp he wore every day. His eyes had adapted to the point he could read by the light of his cigarette. He just felt more comfortable in the dark.

He sat on the side of the bed for awhile to get his balance. His headache was vise-like, interspersed with sharp pains darting from his eyes to the base of his skull, a typical hangover headache. However, he finally summoned enough reserve to get out of the creaky bed and shuffle barefoot over the cold linoleum to the kitchen. The coffee maker had just finished growling. He fumbled on the shelf for a glass and poured it full. Drinking coffee from a glass had been a habit since the age of fourteen. He drank it black and figured people who used cream were wimps, socialites, or non-union. He inhaled the hot aroma and swore there was no more pleasurable smell except that of a woman in heat. The headache became tolerable after the first glass of coffee, and he poured the second.

He finally switched the light on about 5:30 A.M. Light was too revealing. His cuticles were black, and although he had cleaned under his nails the night before, hardened coal dust coalesced there. His swollen knuckles were permanently impregnated with the blackness of millions of years ago, remnants perhaps of a giant fern or a towering conifer. He often wondered if Sarah minded being touched by his tainted hands.

He put on the same pair of pants he had worn yesterday. No use in wearing clean pants every day, he thought. His T-shirt was emblazoned with, "YOUR MAMA IS A COAL MINER." He strained to wiggle his broad, sore feet into his stubborn work boots.

He went to the bathroom to wash his face but couldn't tell any difference afterwards. Most of his pores were pitted black. The image in the mirror was not how he saw himself. Girls called him handsome when he was young, but now his face looked cloned, solemn and craggy, like all the men he worked with. A blue New York Yankee baseball hat hid his thinning hair. He thought he looked at least a decade older than he actually was.

The bedroom seemed cold as he walked in to get his keys. He glanced at Sarah but decided not to awaken her since she had been up late watching Real Life Heroes. She was a fairly good wife, nothing spectacular, just steady. She had produced no children, only four miscarriages and one stillborn. He had fathered a son by his Vietnamese whore during the war, but had never told Sarah, never saw any reason to. He wondered if their childless marriage was punishment for his reckless youth.

It was still dark as he stopped on the porch of his trailer to puff his cigarette. Not a single light was visible anywhere. Venus and a sliver of crescent moon with upturned horns were faintly visible in the eastern sky. A flock of crows were awakening the woods behind the trailer.

His Ford truck of ten years coughed and sputtered almost as badly as he did before it started. He rolled the window open and drove slowly down the mountain road. Driving this way allowed him to experience the smells and sounds. Although his senses of smell and hearing had been dulled somewhat by working in the mines, he tried to experience the world around him to keep his senses as tuned as possible. He attributed his love of the natural world to his part Cherokee heritage. Passing the kudzu patch, he could smell the intense grape fragrance of the blooms. He faintly heard the drumming of a pileated woodpecker, then its eerie call sounding like a misplaced tropical bird. As the curve finally yielded to a straight stretch, Jeb saw a red fox cross the road, but it seemed to be moving in slow motion. He attributed the strange scene to his lingering hangover. He stomped the brakes and fishtailed to a stop for fear of hitting the fox. It was now suspended in the beams of the headlights. He rubbed his eyes, thinking he was hallucinating. Yet when he opened his eyes, the vision of the dangling fox was still there. The fox turned its head and looked directly at Jeb as if to communicate, yet no thoughts were tendered. Jeb blinked his eyes and the fox was gone. His heart was pounding, so he sat there in the truck in the middle of the road trying to calm himself, and wondered about the meaning of what he had just seen. He then drove deliberately on down the road and vaguely remembered his great-grandfather telling him a fox would someday be his spirit animal.

Still shaken, he pulled through the gate of Allegheny Mine #47. For some strange reason he suddenly remembered today was his forty-seventh birthday. As he stepped out of his truck he saw ol' Harv Jones, who had been a good friend for twenty years. "Harv, you believe in omens or bad luck?" he asked.

"Sure don't," said Harv. "Just the opposite. I've never had bad luck unless you count this job and my first two wives. Why, I even keep a black cat chained to a clothes line so it will run across my path every time I leave the house. I've outlived twelve of those suckers, but two of them I stepped on in the dark and squashed."

Jeb laughed and said, "Harv, you're a crazy old goat."

They made small talk as they walked to the mine entrance. Jeb stopped to pet Bituminous, a black mongrel that was considered the mine mascot. He liked Jeb because Jeb occasionally sneaked him a beer. Bituminous had been so drunk he couldn't hold his back leg up to pee.

They flipped on their headlamps and strapped themselves into the cart for the long ride into the guts of the earth. They were to begin mining a new area off the distal part of the main shaft. Even though Jeb was foreman and knew his job well, he was always leery of new shafts. It didn't matter to Harv since he didn't believe in bad luck anyway.

The cart came to a grating halt and the twenty men groaned about another day in the mine. Jeb greeted all the guys on his shift. He asked Dwayne, "Has your wife delivered yet?"

"Sure has, she calved yesterday, an eight pound boy," Dwayne replied. "Big and strong, but he ain't going to be no miner - he's going to college,"

Jeb quipped, "Did you ever find out who the baby's father is?"

"No but we've narrowed it down to about ten guys and you're not one of them, Jeb, because we all know you can't get it up anymore."

"But I could nine months ago," Jeb said. "Besides, your wife has more class than to go to bed with you." Everyone laughed heartily, but half the laughs turned to coughs. "Let's get to work, you rascals."

It took about an hour to reorient the machinery that gnawed away the coal like a fat man at a pie-eating contest.

"Crank her up and let her rip," said Jeb.

The metal monster began ripping away chunks of coal, the noise sounding like a horrific mixture of diesel trucks, giant rattling chains, and a thousand banshees with laryngitis. Jeb respected this steel dragon. Ten years earlier, it had shredded the social finger on his left hand. It continued devouring the dark wall of coal.

After they had cut about fifty feet into the new shaft, Jeb shut the machine off and called for a fifteen-minute break. When the clamor died down, Jeb heard a hissing noise behind him, like steam escaping from a radiator. His heart quickened for the second time today and his breathing deepened. At the instant he tried to say "run," the wall of the mine behind him blew out. Flying chunks of coal from the size of walnut to watermelon flew into him and past him. He saw a large boulder hit Harv in the head and render him immediately unconscious. Dwayne was closest to the explosion and was buried all but one leg. Jeb, in great pain, worked furiously to remove the load of coal from Dwayne's chest and head and breathed a few breaths into his silent lungs. He checked Harv's neck and felt a faint pulse. Only then did Jeb realize they had hit a methane pocket and the gas under pressure had exploded the wall. He didn't know whether the other seventeen men were under the rubble or were far enough back to have missed the explosion. He could feel himself weakening and becoming dizzy. He knew he must sit still and breathe slowly, consume as little of the oxygen and methane mixture as possible. He could think of nothing but the irony of being killed by a pocket of sixty-five million year old gas on his birthday. He struggled to think of Sarah and his son in Vietnam, but could not. He saw a dim vision of a fox in his headlamp and his last remembrance was that of an intense physical pain before he lapsed into unconsciousness. His spiritual body slowly began to uncouple from his lifeless physical form and took with it all the thought processes. It took the body heat and began to rise. Jeb's soul could see the entire scene, but saw it in a very detached way, like it didn't matter what happened. Dwayne's spirit rose from his body and the two souls together turned away from the catastrophe.

Ahead were two dim lights, each of the souls being inextricably drawn to a separate light. Jeb's light grew more intense and he passed through it into the greatest brightness he could ever imagine. This brightness was not just a light but a somebody or a something. He was comfortable here. His dull senses had become extraordinarily acute. The blackness had been cleansed away. He felt a belonging he never wanted to lose. Then his movement through the brightness slowed and the light dimmed. He again felt a racking ache and wondered why there was pain in the hereafter. It dawned on his spirit this might be a prelude to hell. The light again became brighter and now hurt his eyes. He heard his name called, but couldn't tell if it was Satan or God.

"Jeb, Jeb," said the voice in a deep, deep tone.

Jeb thought, "Oh my God, a voice like that has to be the devil's."

"Jeb, can you hear me?" roared the voice again. "It's me, Mongo. You're okay, everything is all right. Everyone's alive." Mongo's headlamp glared directly into Jeb's eyes.

"Mongo, are we in heaven or hell?" Jeb asked.

"We're in hell, Jeb. Some people call it Tennessee, but it has always been hell to me."

When Jeb awoke again he was lying outside the mine on a stretcher, surrounded by onlookers. Bituminous wedged his way in between all the legs and licked Jeb's blackened face.

Jeb said, "Bituminous, I saw Jesus today and he said me and you are going to have to stop drinking and chasing women. I'm coming to get your black butt Sunday and we're going out into the woods for a prayer meeting."

Bituminous whimpered, then raised his left hind leg and peed on the stretcher. He then let out an uncharacteristic howl. Jeb at first thought Bituminous had found salvation, but then understood that was not the case.

"You're worthless, Bituminous. And you're right, it's going to take more than bright lights and prayer meetings to save our no-account souls."

Jeb thought he heard the high-pitched yap of a fox in the distance just before he drifted into a half-sleep.

DAVID K. FENNER is a physician living and practicing medicine in Elizabethton. He is currently working on an action-adventure novel.

Phyllis Gobbell

Firewood

Best wishes to a fellow writer and contributor Phyllis Gobbell

Lottie Poole follows alongside the green pickup as it crawls off the blacktop, pulling into the splotchy grass. It's no use telling her father he can park under the carport. Lottie is never sure how much she can blame on hardening arteries and how much is stubbornness with roots three-quarters of a century old.

The engine creaks and sighs as Lottie meets the truck. She wrestles with the door.

"Did you have any trouble?"

Her father pushes his feet into his work boots. "Not a lick," he says, tugging at the laces with his big, rough hands. He's in no hurry, climbing down from the cab. He has to tuck his Camels in his shirt pocket. He has to drape his work jacket over his arm and give his bright yellow Caterpillar cap a yank. He cranes his neck. "I expected more of a dent in that woodpile." On the side porch is nearly a rick of wood.

Lottie takes hold of her father's arm. She feels hard muscle through the khaki work shirt. He is still lean and tough, still surefooted. He comes to cut firewood for her. She explains, it's not been cold yet. He grunts.

He carries a brown grocery sack with its top folded down so there can't be much in it. Never mind that he owns all sizes of luggage, gifts from Lottie. "Is that all?" she asks.

"Don't take much for me to travel."

Lottie knows how far his travelings have taken him. To Detroit when he was twenty. Across the state to Memphis when his brother was alive. Now and for years, his longest trip has been from Monteagle Mountain to Lottie's house, sixty miles.

"She brought me right on down." He slaps the green hood affectionately. Lottie always marvels, every time this relic from her father's logging days makes it another sixty miles.

"Sounds like she's dying."

"Nah. All she needs is a rest, and she'll be raring to go again." A flash of mischief lights his milky eyes, an expression that cheers Lottie in some unaccountable way.

"You said four o'clock. I was worried."

"Aw, Norma like to never let me get off."

"I bet Norma wants me to call her."

"Prob'ly."

Lottie has to smile, imagining Norma rushing in on a wave of beauty parlor scents, shaking her finger as she preps their father for his trip. Now you must do this and you know you can't do that. Will you remember, Daddy? Do you promise? One more thing. Do have that baby sister of mine call me.

Menopause baby, Norma is forever saying, on that sugary note that means spoiled. Norma is old enough to be Lottie's mother and she has never let her forget she was an accident.

Lottie lets the screen bang behind them. She has to push with her shoulder to close the heavy wood door.

"I can fix that sticking," says her father. "The screen, too. It shouldn't flap like that. Where do you want this?" He holds out his sack, like someone else's garbage.

Lottie leads him back to the room he occupies every time. "Make yourself at home," she says, knowing he will behave like a guest. A guest waits to be shown his room. Guests do not park under the carport.

"I ought to bring in my saw," he says, his wiry brows lifting suddenly. He raises his cap and scratches. His iron-gray hair is thinner. "I bought a new chain."

"Rest a minute," Lottie says. Nobody's going to steal his saw in broad daylight, but her father's heavy steps on the hardwood floor sound with unmistakable resolve.

He opens the front door with one powerful tug. "I'll put it on the porch." He examines the screen door. "Spring must be broke. I'll fix that tomorrow."

The sun hangs so low over the pug-nosed pickup, Lottie has to squint. Her father takes a very long time piddling at his truck. Rattling, scraping noises come from the bed. A black Toyota passes by him, dangerously close. Lottie's breath catches. She thinks of the rush of wind on his back and squeezes her own slight arms. Her father throws up his hand in a neighborly greeting.

He brings his yellow McCulloch to the porch, carrying it in a box like a pet, and sets it behind a planter of dried-up marigolds. He raises the bill of his cap and blows out a long breath.

"Come inside," Lottie says. She insists. She uses her school-teacher voice, and he obeys.

"I didn't bring my gas can to the porch," he says, standing at the kitchen sink, filling a glass with water from the tap. "Might be a danger of fire."

Lottie pulls a chair back from the table. "Here. Rest while I finish supper."

"Nah." He gulps the water, his Adam's-apple sliding up and down. The skin hangs loose on his long neck. He sighs noisily and wipes his mouth on his sleeve. "I ought to look around outside, see what trees are down. So I'll be ready to cut wood in the morning, bright and early."

"Dad-dy," Lottie begins. Her tinny voice startles her. What she hears is Norma. She doesn't finish. He's not listening anyway.

Lottie's father has always kept her in firewood.

It has been more than a decade since she and Clark bought the old rambling farm house, vowing to use the fireplace for heat, to save energy. Clark worked for the County Department of Conservation. Now he is somewhere in

California saving redwoods with another woman. Lottie realizes she was pulled along by Clark's convictions. She didn't mind as long as he loved her.

In the fall after the first frost, Lottie's father would drive down Monteagle Mountain with his McCulloch in his pickup, cut wood, bust it, haul it, stack it. He'd stand back, looking proud, and Clark would ask, "How much do I owe you?" Clark always pouted when his father-in-law refused money. Gratitude was hard for Clark.

Lottie's father gave the same sharp answer every time: "I can do this much for my daughter."

Last year he made five trips to her house. Lottie dropped fifteen pounds when Clark left. She gave her math classes excessive assignments and spent evenings and weekends grading papers in front of the fireplace, her quilt draped around her thin shoulders, Indian-style. Dustballs accumulated under the furniture. Lottie tossed her underthings across chairs and left food in dishes to dry up and stink.

"You have plenty of firewood," her father would say, speaking into the flames, his voice hollow and helpless. "I can keep you in wood."

There was so much wood. The side porch sagged. She kept telling other teachers at her school, Take all you can use.

But she had the fire, that much. In the big, drafty house, so empty after Clark left, Lottie slept in the chair near the fireplace, comforted by the spewing and crackling and the rhythm of the flames. Down in her bones nothing could warm her, but she did not have to go to her cold bed.

Lottie finally phones her sister. "No trouble," she says. "He's checking the property for fallen trees."

"Oh, Sweet Jesus, thank you, I can finally breathe an easy breath," Norma moans.

Lottie winces, guilty for dawdling while Norma worried. Guilty once more.

"He didn't tell you, did he? I said, 'Have Lottie call me the minute you get there, Daddy, you know I'll be wringing my hands.' He forgot, didn't he? This is what I mean. I have to stay after him. He says I'm a fussy old hen, but somebody has to think about his welfare. I pleaded with him, 'Let me put you on the bus, Daddy. You can take your blessed chain saw on the bus.' He's so mule-headed. Do you see what I've been telling you?"

Lottie hedges. If she waits, Norma may answer her own question.

"The truth, Lottie. Can't you tell he's failing?"

The sun has gone behind the dark trees and left a reddish, purplish patch in the sky, like a huge bruise. Lottie wishes her father would come in.

She says, "He seems well to me."

"Seems well?" Norma's laugh is brittle.

"You worry too much, Norma. Come on, turn the worrying over to me for this one weekend. I'll give him back Sunday. Enjoy the break. You and Lyle take a bottle of champagne to the jaccuzi and make mad, passionate love."

The crackle of a poor connection is the only sound on the line. Lottie moves up to the window. The curly telephone cord slides through her fingers.

"You're very funny," Norma says at last. "Well, that's our little Lottie. Light-hearted, carefree Lottie. Like a little butterfly. Sometimes you got on Mamma's nerves when you were too flippant, but you always charmed Daddy."

"Menopause baby." Lottie gets the jump on Norma.

"Exactly. Why should I expect any different? Please don't mistake what I'm saying for jealousy, Lottie. For all the burden Daddy is now, we've had our times. After Mamma died, before this other business, the disease. We were two adults with respect for each other. I liked it that way. So don't misunderstand."

"Dad's coming in, Norma." Lottie watches the lanky figure moving along the fence row. He tosses the butt of his Camel. Lottie wonders if it's still burning on the ground. She waits for her father to climb on the fence and swing his leg over, take a short cut.

"Get him to show you his skinned elbow, Lottie. I went over to fix his supper and his shirt was ripped at the elbow, all bloody. He didn't remember what happened. These little things - you don't have the faintest notion, Lottie. He's worse than a child. I could make a child do."

Lottie watches her father go all the way to the gate.

Norma's voice is unexpectedly earnest. "What if he drives off the mountainside? What if he falls on his chain saw while he's cutting your wood? You don't worry about those things, do you?"

"I'll take good care of him, Norma."

Norma gives a big phony laugh. "Who's taking care of who? That's what I want to know. Do you really need wood that bad, Lottie?"

"Does Norma fix your supper every night?" Lottie asks, after he's picked at the chicken and rice and steamed veggies.

"Most nights. She flies in, flies out. Swishes that feather duster. Sprays that Lysol. Never sits, that girl." Suddenly he asks, "You ever hear from Clark?"

"No."

"He's still out west, I reckon."

"As far as I know. Really, I don't care." Lottie takes a swipe across the table with the dishrag, glaring to make her point.

"Your mamma said, 'Lottie will whittle down Clark Poole's big notions.' Me, I never trusted him. Take the thing about wood. He was set on using wood heat. Now he's gone to saving trees. I don't see his point."

"Dad-"

"You'll meet some nice fella yet," he says gently.

"Ah yes, Marshall County is so overrun with prospects." Lottie catches herself and wonders why she said such a thing. She is not looking for a man, cannot imagine skin-to-skin, not yet.

Lottie's father comes to the sink and drops his glass in the dishwater. "This place is a lot of upkeep for a woman by herself."

"I do all right. It's just such a big barny house."

"Get one of them wood-burning stoves." Her father's voice trails as he goes to the back door, reaching for his Camels. "I can keep you in wood."

Later he squats at the fireplace and builds a one-match fire. He is meticulous in arranging his kindling with wadded newspaper, stacking his logs. The paper flames, smoke boils out from the logs. The wood catches, the chimney sucks up the smoke. Lottie's father nods. "Good-drawing chimney."

His bones creak as he sits in the easy chair. "Now don't let me knock you out of anything. Don't use me as no excuse, either. I came to cut wood, that's all." He takes out his glasses and shakes open the county weekly. He angles the lamp and holds the paper just so.

Lottie pulls a rocking chair close to the fire. "Dad, let me help you cut wood tomorrow."

Her father raises his eyes sharply. "That's foolishness."

"It is not foolishness."

"I couldn't work with you under foot, girl. I wouldn't have it."

Lottie stokes the fire. The night creeps on, crawls toward eight o'clock. Her father reads every line, chuckling from time to time. He turns to the advertisements, last page.

Lottie stands with her back to the fireplace. Her legs bake through her jeans. She feels shivery and fragile. "Dad, tell me the truth. Was I an accident?"

Her father folds the paper. He winks. "More like a surprise." He grins, shakes his head. Whatever he's remembering, it is his own secret.

By eight o'clock he has dozed off in his chair. He breathes in, snorting, and blows out the corner of his dry, thin lips. A shock of hair meant to lie across his head sprouts the other way. Lottie bends over him. She watches his nearly-transparent eyelids fluttering lightly. One of his fingernails is mashed black. She wonders if Norma missed that. Probably not. With her fingertips, Lottie brushes her father's unruly hair into place.

Lottie fixes bacon and eggs and canned biscuits for his breakfast.

"Norma rolls out the dough at night and leaves me a pan of biscuits ready for the oven," her father says. He frowns at Lottie's toast. "That don't stick to your ribs."

The early light shimmers on the air. "Light frost," he says, stepping onto the porch, letting the screen door flap. "A fine day for work."

He walks to the edge and points with his Camel between his thumb and forefinger. "There's a dead poplar over yonder. Down the fence row. Easy to get the truck in from the road, get the wood out."

"Be careful," Lottie tells him when he goes. "Please be careful."

After a time, she hears the power saw crank up. The noise is familiar, spurts of groaning, her father juicing it. It is sometime later that the ferocious whine makes a connection in her brain: There's a dead poplar over yonder.

Lottie knows a tree is coming down.

She pulls on her boots and sweater. She thinks of all the hundreds of trees her father has felled in his time, but it does not ease her as she runs in the brown grass between the black-top and the fence row.

Not far off, Lottie's father stands with trembly legs spraddled, wielding the yellow McCulloch as it strains to a high pitch. The saw grinds its teeth into the center of the dead tree, spitting out a spray of fine chips, and Lottie can tell from the set of her father's back and shoulders, it takes everything he's got.

The saw chews out the last of the wedge from the trunk.

Lottie hangs on the fence.

The tree topples with a mighty Cr-rack!

Her father yells, "Lordy!"

He lets the weight of the chain saw pull him with it, going down on one knee, head bent, shoulders hunched forward. His whole body moves with his hard breathing. Lottie holds her breath.

He comes out of his jacket. He pulls his handkerchief from his pocket and presses it against his face, mopping sweat. The back of his shirt is soaked. He takes his cap off his plastered-down hair.

Somewhere a twig snaps, the only sound in the woods. Lottie's father is as still as the poplar that lies before him.

He raises his eyes, gazing at the tree in fear or perhaps in wonder. Lottie knows one thing: he won't quit till he has her firewood. It is all she can do, to do nothing. She slips away. Somewhere along the fence row she hears the power saw start up.

"This load oughta do you," her father says. "You won't need no more for a while."

He has carefully aligned the back bumper with the porch. He comes down from the cab with sawdust stuck to his face, sawdust falling from the cuffs of his pants. He brushes sawdust from his sleeves before he reaches into his shirt pocket for his Camels. The back of his hand is raw, the skin scraped off.

"This is plenty," Lottie tells him.

"I didn't get it all busted."

"Don't worry about it. Please. This is fine."

He smells of gasoline and sweat, mingled with the heavy, sappy-sweet odor of the wood. "Let me clean up that nasty hand, Dad."

"Nah. I could use a glass of water." He does not look at Lottie. He lights his cigarette and takes a long draw. His eyes, fixed on the wood, seem glazed-over.

Lottie brings a glass. Now her father is stacking her

firewood, going at it hard, putting too much into a job that never looked hard for him before. Lottie wants to see his upper body swing. She wants his fluid motions back. She cannot bear it that he's an old man.

"I didn't get into the trunk. This is all limbs," he says, apologetically. The sticks of firewood bump against the house with a sound of urgency.

"It's a good load, Dad. Don't worry about it. Here, drink your water."

Finally he stops, wipes his face with his sleeve. "Burn the dry first."

"I will."

Then he says, "I got to get on home."

"Today?"

"Soon as I finish up here. I got to get back."

"Dad-dy-"

"This'll do." There is a snap to her father's voice when a thing is final, and all Lottie can do is hold out a glass of water to him.

PHYLLIS GOBBELL is a Tennessee native and has served on the board of the Tennessee Writers Alliance since its inception. She works part-time as a technical writer and teaches classes in writing, and her most recent short story appeared in Tennessee's bicentennial anthology, *Home Works*. She resides in Nashville.

Connie Jordan Green

A Gardener's Year

*Congratulations —
and best wishes
to my fellow writer.
Connie*

Hands, knees, and backs know Tennessee's seasons—seasons spent in the garden.

SPRING

For a gardener, the year begins in March, if the steady cycling of seasons can be said to have either ending or beginning. On the first pleasant day, we step from the cocoon of our winter houses to find the lawn littered with limbs, each nook and corner filled with dead leaves—winter's debris a blot on what we want clean, green, shining with newness and life.

Outdoor chores have no end. Still, we make a start, so that when the center of the sun stands directly over the equator, marking a day and night equal in length all over the earth, we will be ready, not only in spirit, as we're always ready for spring, but also to be underway with our work.

In the garden, wobbly green lines of early peas cross the rich, black earth. Nearby, lettuce spreads a frilly green carpet. In another quadrant, short stems and small leaves of broccoli and cabbage hint at the umbrella-like plants to come.

Things are no quieter in the flower beds. Although the last freeze bowed low jonquils that had dared to bloom, others have not been discouraged. Their yellow trumpets call green tips of hyacinth and tulip from the earth. The brightest splash of color comes from the pansies, their upturned faces of yellow, purple, and white regarding me with amusement as I go about my chores.

114

Wildflowers, too, have declared spring. Hepatica, noticing the lengthening daylight, dotted the woods with white, blue, and purple blossoms, when to venture forth seemed folly. Others soon followed suit—bloodroot, toothwort, violets, spring beauty—all responding to an internal clock set eons ago by a world where spring's return is a certainty, despite the daily capriciousness of weather.

By the first full week of spring, even the patient trees are eager, their urge toward blossom and leaf held in check only by cold nights. Maples, tinged with red along the hillsides, will soon be a burst of color. By mid-April, ridges will be patch-worked green—shading from the chartreuse of poplars to the truer green of wild cherry and sumac into the emerald of pine and cedar, all counterpointed by the antique lace of stately oaks, dressed in beige splendor, head and shoulders above lesser trees.

Like other gardeners, I attempt to control some of this green abundance. Maple seedlings carpet lawn, garden, and flower beds. They spring up between the bricks along the sidewalks and in the center of the driveway. They sprout in gutters and flower pots. Only hand-pulling will thwart their desire to out-survive the rest of the world.

Fields, too, have greened, and all around the chug of tractors is part of spring's melody. Birds would drown out the tractors if they had sufficient volume. They have ample numbers. For several weeks birds have been staking out their territory, gathering nesting materials, surveying the area where they'll spend the next months. The business of preparing for a family energizes the birds, and they sing in time with their efforts.

Gardening is humbling work. Not only does the miracle of growth leave one in awe, but also, because bending is hard on the back and squatting wrecks the knees, one spends hours kneeling. It's not a bad angle from which to view the world.

In early May I crawl about in the strawberry patch, battling two grass enemies—Bermuda and crab. Bermuda moves in clumps just beneath the surface. I push my digging fork into them, work the tines down among the knots, and tug out a handful. They are sturdy and stringy enough that if I pull carefully, I can usually clean out all traces.

Crab grass is less cooperative, sending underground shoots in all directions. Only its green leaves make the roots easy to locate. I dig carefully alongside the grass blades, trying not to sever the tender roots. Then I lift the root, dislodging a foot or more when I'm lucky.

Nearby the vegetable garden waits, crab grass slipping long fingers, Bermuda grass knotting beneath the bordering trench I try to keep clean. Through spring, well into the heat of summer, I crawl among the vegetables, fruits, and flowers, occasionally glancing up at the world around me, knowing whose garden this really is and what my part is in the scheme of things.

SUMMER

At Stonehenge the sun is setting over the most northwestern stone. Here in Tennessee I mark the summer solstice by climbing the cherry tree, basket in hand, and picking those fruits the birds have spared. I feel lucky to garner a pie's worth, the birds keeping a closer eye than I.

June is a month of aromas—honeysuckle and roses, freshly mowed hay, and scents from the herb bed—thyme, basil, sage. Morning is best for appreciating the nose-bouquets, arising early an easy chore in summer. Unfortunately, such mornings are numbered. That's the downside of the summer solstice. Granted, summer days were numbered from the start, but as long as I saw a minute or two of daylight added with each successive day, I convinced myself summer stretched on and on. Now, as they say, the handwriting is on the wall.

Or on the calendar.

Blackberries are constantly on my mind in July, a gift from the gods with strings attached.

Several years ago, my sister planted hybrid blackberries on her suburban lot. Thornless, they grew lush, large berries. I picked and ate, but my soul wasn't satisfied. Only a trip into the wild blackberry brambles supplied the missing essence. Skin and clothing assaulted by thorns and bugs, I knew summer had come.

Part of the attraction is the fact blackberries grow free and abundant. They fed bugs, bears, and small animals long before we came. They'll do so again when we vanish. Meanwhile, we borrow their goodness, at no cost except some sweat and toil.

Part of the appeal is that picking blackberries evokes rich childhood memories. My dad was a picker extraordinaire. With a pail buckled around his waist, his hands flew through the briars. My sisters and I helped him—or so we thought. Mostly we complained about thorns, bugs, and heat, while we ate more berries than we put in our pails.

An acquaintance, knowing I had been blackberry picking, asked if I would sell some. I would—for a hundred dollars a gallon. Even joy has its price.

The strainer and pressure canner have taken up residence in my kitchen. All winter they hide out on a basement shelf, but come summer and fruits and vegetables, they assume the role of honored guests.

Fruit goes into the top of the strainer, peels and discards come out one side, and usable juice or pulp pours down a chute. It is the ultimate time-saving invention in my summer kitchen. The canner, of course, makes food safe for consumption next winter.

Nature has been on a productive kick—or since fruits contain plant seeds, I suppose it's a reproductive kick. Tomatoes have begun their wild gallop to cover every vine with rich, red fruit. If they're pursuing the apple crop, trying to match it in vigor, they have a ways to go. The thud of apples hitting the well house roof or falling onto the ground accompanies my outdoor chores.

The trees my family set out during our early years on the farm now spread into one another, some limbs reaching toward the sky, some drooping so with fruit that I must stoop to mow beneath them. They are winesap, red and gold delicious, and an old apple a friend grafted from a tree that was weathered and gnarled when we bought our farm 33 years ago. That original tree bowed to a wind storm some years back, but the healthy grafted tree produces large yellow apples with distinctive red strips running from stem to blossom end.

Summer is about abundance. A friend told me once she didn't like to plant a garden because it was feast or famine. I always thought that was the blessing of gardens; vines weighted with cucumbers, a crowd of tomatoes showing their rosy cheeks between green leaves, zucchinis stretching inches overnight (now there's a vegetable we ignore at our own peril), fingers of green beans massed among the stems.

Admittedly, there are times when picking, preparing, and preserving get to be too much, when fall frost sounds like a blessing. But that day won't come for another month. July's business is to garden and to enjoy every moment — cool early mornings, flowers and leaves tipped with dew, grass wet beneath our feet; tidy garden rows where we've pulled weeds; a basket heaped with fresh vegetables and fruits; jars filled with jewel tones lining the shelves, summer's gifts becoming winter's treasures, the garden going on with its giving year-round.

It's that time of year again — the garden has more weeds and bugs than vegetables, flowering plants are leggy and unenthusiastic about blooming, and by late morning the heat and humidity drive us to close the windows and turn on the air conditioner. I walk around the garden, think of the effort required to make things look right, then sit on the porch with a glass of lemonade.

August it's-not-worth-the-effort has started.

Mother Nature seems to feel the same way. I've seen some of her impatience to move on to another season. Last week I found a fallen walnut, its hull yellowish-brown and firm. The mitten-like leaves of sassafras are turning orange, forecasting the red that will follow. Dogwood berries, having gone from green to yellow to orange, now impinge on red.

Doves know summer is almost gone. Early morning and late evening they coo their mournful song, saying farewell to long, hot days. Some of the wildlife that surrounds my house doesn't seem to care if August never ends. Groundhogs, in particular, are glad for this year's abundant fruit crop. They not only steal tomatoes from the garden and feast on fallen apples, but, boldened, they come to the kitchen door and peer in at me.

I suppose next they'll want to sit at the table. If August goes on much longer, I may invite them in.

FALL

We've known for weeks it was coming—that day when fall is truly here, leaves showing their crimson-orange-yellow hues, the sky blue, the air crisp and smelling of tangy apples. It happened with a weather front moving through, clearing out the hottest temperatures, the haziest air.

Husband Dick and I are happy at this time of year with our sloppy farming habits which allow wildly overgrown fence rows to crisscross the farm. Those rows blaze with red and orange maples, maroon dogwoods, red sumac and sassafras, yellow redbud, and a host of other trees in assorted colors.

The colors are especially beautiful in contrast with the neatly mowed green fields, an area where we are tidier.

Much as I'm loathe to give such a villain credit, I have to admit one of the prettiest fall sights is poison ivy. It grows on the back wall of our barn, where late-day sun slants, painting a picture worthy of an artist's brush.

I suppose everything has its value—the summer-sweet smell of honeysuckle bloom to offset the vine's peskiness, the autumn brilliance of poison ivy leaves to compensate for the itchy fits inflicted by contact with the plant.

Nature evens things out her own way.

Despite the apparent slide into dormancy by most of nature, autumn is no time for humans to become slothful.

The garden may fall asleep unaided, but it's up to us to tuck it in. The wind-driven rattle of corn stalks admonishes us for being late with our chores. Okra, finally subdued by frost, clings stubbornly to the soil. Pulling okra stalks is back-breaking exercise. Dick and I pull and haul away, run the bush-hog through the remaining weeds, and tuck the garden in with a blanket of leaves.

Not only the vegetable garden, but also all the flower beds need plant matter removed and a heavy mulch applied. This covering-up of the gardens involves an uncovering of the rest of our hilltop. Leaf raking is a never-ending chore. The same leaves that were so beautiful a few weeks ago now shower down, burying shrubbery and lawn. One good rain and they become a heavy, soggy layer that smothers grass and disfigures shrubbery. So we rake—a chore that continues until January's cold, miserable weather drives us indoors.

Pruning is another fall chore—shaping up the boxwoods and junipers, getting rid of tree limbs that interfere with mowing, cutting trees that encroach upon the hilltop. With the latter chore we achieve two goals, the second being to enlarge the woodpile.

Only nature can afford a rest during this season.

November may lack shade and shine, butterflies and bees, but it doesn't lack seeds. They appear in every conceivable size and shape—round, oblong, triangular, rectangular, narrow and hooked, coiled and spiral, winged or horned, lighter than air or heavy enough to raise a lump if one falls on us. They stick to jackets and shoes, ride into the house on pant legs and socks, abundant evidence of nature's desperation to guarantee propagation.

I spend hours picking from our clothing the small, flat, triangular seeds we call beggar's lice. Stick-tights, with their needle-like horns that hook onto fabric, are equally aggravating. They remain from the beautiful black-eyed Susans we admired a few weeks ago. Burrs, too, are annoying, not terrible on clothing but almost impossible to remove from the long-haired cats and dogs. Fur wraps around the burrs, forming a knot that only scissors can eliminate.

Yet, for all we fuss about the nuisance, our world would soon vanish without seeds. They are the means whereby most of life on earth reproduces itself, and they feed much of the animal kingdom.

Nature's cycle is remarkable—a fact I have to acknowledge even while I pick more than my share of that cycle off jeans and socks.

WINTER

It isn't going to get any darker. That's the good news of the winter solstice. We have seen the worse. Now we're on the upswing.

Hope provides our winter sun, hope and a mailbox filled with seed catalogs, those publications lush with purple prose and pictorial edens. Anything seems possible when seed catalogs are spread before me—flowers that bloom on and on, remaining compact and vigorous; corn that grows multiple ears, sweet as candy; squash and watermelon that swell ripely, resistant to the wilt that invades my summer garden.

In seed catalogs there are neither bugs nor drought, high winds nor hail storms. Browsing seed catalogs is near enough to Shangri-La or Camelot. Sufficient unto the day are the pleasures thereof.

Our pleasures are in small things—another few minutes

of daylight each week, dreams of spring and growth and warmth suffusing our bodies and souls, comfort to get us through winter.

Sunlight creeps toward the corner of the house. In a few days it'll sneak a ray onto the screened porch, teasing us with promises of sunny evenings spent in the glider. Increasing daylight turns on not only us humans, but all nature. Even the cats, who I thought could sleep away the rest of their lives, now frisk about the yard, running up trees and leaping onto the wellhouse, chasing one another beneath the bird feeder.

The fruit trees, which I managed to prune in due time last month, stand starkly against the blue sky, branches spread wide, waiting for blossom and fruit. Winter is occasionally kind to gardeners, here and there giving us a day of warmth and sun in which to tackle the garden. On each such day we've dug, hauled, trimmed, weeded, planted, and transplanted.

Never mind that major snowstorms and the blizzard of the century have occurred in March and early April. We live with confidence that spring comes in earnest after February. All nature's signs lead us to this conviction. Right on time the Lenten Rose bloomed, its deep pink flowers opening with the Mardi Gras celebrations. Not to be outdone, jonquils waved their cups of yellow, and crocus shyly hugged the ground with white and purple flowers.

The woods, too, got in on the act, quietly announcing spring's emergence. White bloodroot and toothwort and pale blue hepatica flowers dot the hillsides.

An important song of spring has begun, maybe the most convincing of all the signs of the season. On Saturday while I planted the last of the peas, I heard peepers, their cries rising from the low part of the pasture. Peepers are a certain harbinger of warmer weather. They know winter is all but done, even if she does give us a nasty surprise occasionally.

Nature has done her part. Only the calendar is left to declare spring and the onset of another gardening year.

Connie Jordan Green

Leaving Eden

Perhaps it happened
in September, here —

the two figures,
backs to the green garden,
stumbling over rocks —

the hillsides
suddenly wounded
with the bruised hues of fall —

the two awake for the first time
to the ghastly beauty of decay.

CONNIE JORDAN GREEN has written extensively in the past for chil-
dren. Her novel, *The War at Home*, was named one of the *ALA Best
Books for Young Adults*, and *Emmy* was a *Notable 1992 Children's Trade
Book in the Field of Social Studies*. Both books were nominated to the
Volunteer State Book Award Master List. She lives in Lenoir City.

Georganne Harmon

Bluebird Boxes

"That's a good man," you said
of the farmer, who, tilling his vegetable plot,
nodded his head and lifted an index finger
as we passed—"He put out bluebird boxes,"

And I thought of you, who
gather home ancient fence posts,
nail a box you've made
to bluebird specs, train
a vine of clematis to its base.

Now, away, sea salt prickling my skin,
my feet toughened on hot sand,
I swell with this remembering
of how you are, emotion like a wave forming
underneath ocean's glass surface,
a force that gathers without breaking—

I grew and drank the green curves
of Tennessee farms and woods,
like gifts from you, like when we began:
spring locusts dressed for wedding
in nodding white blossoms, scarlet
tanager on a roadside fence—

until the surge crests,
like a breaker in the smooth push of water
that shatters on the sand shore
in separate drops, foamy with air.

Georganne Harmon

Outsider II

Mount Zion Church

I

I jumped out of my skin when her grief
shook pew and somber light and me and
dust motes floating between us—the woman
behind me in her black hat, silk Sunday dress,
belted below full bosom that bellowed
a deep and gathering shriek, slapped
me into it, made flow my pale tears
with her shadowy ones.

Marva said, "I forgot to tell you. We scream."
Mount Zion African Methodist Church did not move
from its foundation, but filled and embraced
the grief that swayed and shouted in its arms
in defiance of that Judge who closes the casket
and ends all hope. That fierce Opponent will cow
a mother, sister, wife, a child who weeps,
but not this woman behind me, not
the preacher's wife, not me (the stranger),
nor the neighbor in the straw hat,
the great-eyed boy. They sway, build
a rhythm of gall, let it gather in their gut,
until it forms an army like Scottish bagpipers
and Indian warriors terrifying in high-pitched,
child-mad attack. Like Hannibal with elephants,
Sister Florence and Brother Jake,
Reverend Hopkins and Mrs. Ford,
they shout down fear with angry heat, and
with their noise make paths of silence
in the shafts of light.

I learn much about writing from your strong, distinctive voices! Best to you. Georganne Harmon

125

II
I remember how, after my grandmother's death
grief took a slow journey through decorum
until it knotted around itself and grew
into hard muscle bound up into haunting guilt—
ablution unperformed that glowered
and called from the dark.

III
At Sunday dinner, my father, having had enough
of women's gossip, commanded more than once,
"Let's talk about roses," his plea an escape
to restraint and grace, for perfume of apple blossoms
in the whipping wind of storm. Unable to scream
out of this Anglo-Saxon skin I live in,
I remember his words when gray moves in or fury
creeps under my fingernails like exotic torture:
I think of spring with its wet dirt, green smells,
hyacinths under the maple in March's light snow.
These visions glaze the dark moods and bring me
short smiles. But all the while, now,
I'm listening for the woman behind me
who shifted dust particles and knocked
the hurt loose in the sad and angry air.

GEORGANNE HARMON has lived in Nashville for most of her life, and has taught in Metro Nashville public schools for twenty years. She currently teaches English at Hume-Fogg Academic High School. Her poems have appeared in *Pearl*, *Potato Eyes*, *Number One*, and *Appalachian Voices*.

Stuart Harris

Starter Jacket

Best of luck in all your new starts
— Stuart Harris

I got this brand new jacket. My momma took me to Target to buy it this past Monday after school. It's what they call a Starter Jacket. The only ones they had in my size was the Oakland Raiders and the New Orleans Saints. I chose the Raiders. I don't know nobody who plays for the Raiders, but it's an awesome jacket. It has this picture of a mean-looking pirate under the team's name. I got it because I throwed my old denim jacket away last weekend on a church retreat. It's hanging on a tree outside a cabin up in the mountains near Gatlinburg.

Most times, the other kids would've gone on the retreat without me. Usually, I have to stay home and work in the garage with my dad. It's like last summer. All the other kids got to go to Camp Linden for a week, canoeing on the Buffalo River and stuff. Later, they even went to Six Flags and a Braves game, stayed in a motel in Atlanta. A bunch of 'em got saved last summer too. About six was baptized the week after they got home from Camp Linden. The church had a special service and made this huge big deal out of it. My mother kept looking at me during the whole service, like she was expecting me to act some special way or something. On the way home in the car, she kept asking stuff like whether I enjoyed the service and didn't I feel kind of left out.

I stayed home the whole summer and worked in my dad's garage. I don't mind the work. In fact, I kind of like changing the oil in cars, charging batteries, and all that. I know more about cars than most men already. And my dad plays cool music all day long, rock and roll. My momma don't like it much, but it just seems to fit with fixing cars.

Anyway, last summer I kept feeling like my friends and me was getting farther and farther apart. I only got to see my best friend Walter on Sundays, in sunday school and church. Then school started and that seemed to cement the deal. We're ninth graders now, at the big high school, almost two thousand kids there, and it ain't like middle school at all. They got us all in these special classes. Walter's an honors student, and he goes around with all his honors student friends all day, taking algebra and French and a bunch of other stuff that'll never do him a bit of good. I'm taking what they call fundamental classes. I'm in reading, math, and a course called Career Education. Best of all, though, I get to take Auto Mechanics. So far I know everything they're teaching in there, but it's still fun to get to work on cars at school. And the older kids, the juniors and seniors, tell me it gets better as you go. I've got one class with Walter, P.E. But, even in there, he hangs out with his honors buddies, and I hang out with the vocational students. Sometimes there's some name-calling back and forth between the groups—"nerds" and "retards"—but Walter and me don't do that, not usually.

The thing that got me on the retreat last weekend was that I got in trouble at school. Mr. Dunham, our reading teacher, was called to the office to talk with the principal. Something about the wrestling schedule, I think. Anyway, we was just sitting there in class playing spades when Luther Duffield got this idea of breaking into Mr. Dunham's cabinet and stealing the wrestling money. Everybody in class knew he kept it in there because these mat girls, prissy honors students, most of 'em, keep coming to his door and paying for their uniforms. Every time, he unlocks that cabinet and puts the money in a little green box he keeps in there.

I didn't like the idea, but I didn't want to look all stuck up either, so I went along with it. Luther was able to pick the lock and get the money. He was just taking it out of the green box when the lookout whispered that Mr. Dunham was coming. Before I knew it, Luther had shoved all the money into my hand and closed the cabinet door. I put it in my old jacket pocket.

We didn't get caught, and Mr. Dunham didn't seem to suspect nothing. We just read aloud like we always do in that class. Sitting there with all that money in my pocket and reading *Sounder* 'til the bell rang was awful. I felt like Mr. Dunham was staring at me the whole time. He asked me to read a paragraph aloud, but my reading was so bad that all of the other kids laughed, and finally Mr. Dunham finished the paragraph for me. After the bell rang, he patted me on the shoulder and said, "Keep your chin up, Kid. You're doing fine." I didn't say nothing, just stood there with my hands crammed down in my pockets. All I wanted was to get out of that room.

During break, I put the money in my locker. Two hours later, Mr. Dunham and the principal was at the door of my Auto Mechanics class, and I knew I was done for. They made me go and unlock my locker, and there wasn't any use pretending I was surprised or making any excuses with all that money staring me in the face. I told them that it was all Luther's idea and that he had passed the money off to me at the last second. He said he had nothing to do with it, but he still got suspended for three days. I was suspended for five days and got a citation for juvenile court.

Going home was a whole 'nother story. They called my dad at the shop, and he came and picked me up. He lectured and cussed in the car the whole way home. At home, my momma was crying, and that was a lot worse than my dad's cussing. Before long, she was blaming herself: maybe if she'd prayed more I never would've stolen that money, and so forth. Then she started into blaming my dad. If I'd gone to church camp instead of working in that garage and listening to rock and roll all summer, I might have found Jesus instead of taking to stealing. I had to sit there listening to all of that. The end of it all was that I got to go on that retreat to Gatlinburg instead of working in the garage last weekend.

On Saturday morning, the sun was just rising over the trees across the valley from our cabin.

"Hey, Walter, look at that," I whispered, pointing to the sunrise and elbowing him in the ribs.

"Shh, not now," he mouthed. Mr. Kendall, the youth director, was saying a prayer as part of our morning devotional before we all went into Gatlinburg for the day. When he finished praying, he said, "Now turn to Page 17 in our songbooks." We sang "He's Everything to Me" out of these little *Sing and Celebrate* books. The singing wasn't much, not like the singing at church when all the adults sing "He Lives" or "He Keeps Me Singing."

> *Jesus, Jesus, Jesus,*
> *Sweetest name I know,*
> *Fills my ev'ry longing,*
> *Keeps me singing as I go.*

I love that song, 'specially when my momma sings this real high part on the last verse, way up above all the rest. She calls it a descant. She sings solos, too: "His Eye is on the Sparrow" and "How Great Thou Art." The songs in that little orange paperback book with these teenagers singing on the front just ain't that good, and we were kind of sleepy anyway.

When we finished our devotional, we ate breakfast. I finished in a hurry. All the kids were talking, but none of 'em was talking to me. I guess everybody knowed what'd happened to me. After about ten minutes, I pushed away from the table, nudged Walter on the elbow, and asked him, "You wanna help me change the tire on that van?" We had a flat coming up the mountain the night before, and Mr. Kendall asked me if I'd put the spare on in the morning.

Walter paused a second, dropped his fork on his plate, and said, "Yeah, sure."

We walked over to the coat rack beside the sliding glass door. There was ice on the door. I put on my jacket, but it hung open because the zipper didn't zip all the way anymore. It didn't look all that good anyway because there was grease stains from the garage all around the pockets. Walter looked at me like I was an orphan. When we opened the door to go out onto the deck, a blast of cold air hit us in the face. We must've left the door open a little too long because someone inside yelled, "Eddie, shut the door. We're freezing in here."

It had snowed just enough the night before to leave a dusting on the trees and the van. The right front tire of the van was flat, and we stood looking at it with our hands in our pockets. "Dern, it's cold out here. Let's hurry and get this thing done," Walter said. I pulled the top of my jacket closed, but it wouldn't stay. I started looking for two big rocks, and Walter opened the back door of the van to get the jack. After I stuck rocks behind the rear wheels, I found a level place to put the jack and raised the jack to the bumper.

While I checked to see that the jack was straight up and down, Walter blew on his cold hands, trying to keep them warm. "Go back inside," I said. "I can finish this up myself."

He looked toward the cabin, then said, "No, if we work together this shouldn't take long." We took turns raising the bumper, pushing the cold metal tire iron with our red hands. We should've brung gloves with us to the mountains, but when we left Nashville the day before, it was a nice fall day. While I switched the flat tire and spare, I began to feel close to Walter again, like me and him was fighting the cold together. I was looking for a way to get him talking to me, the way he used to.

"Walter, you don't think I stole that money, do you?"

"No. You were just with the wrong people, I guess."

I stared into the tires, tightening the lug nuts. "Yeah, that's it. The worst part of all was going home and seeing my momma crying." I turned and looked at Walter. "Walter, you know how you said if we worked together this wouldn't take long."

"Yeah, I was right, wasn't I?"

"Well, I've got a real good feeling about this retreat, but

me and you better stick together like glue."

"Yeah," he said, "We'll probably have a real good time in Gatlinburg today." He picked up the flat tire, holding it with both hands, and leaned it against his thighs. He waddled to the back of the van while I started lowering the bumper. When he got back, I was through. As we put the jack away, Walter put his hand on my shoulder. "Eddie," he said, "You're all right. I'm sure glad you came on this retreat." The way he said it made me feel like a little kid, and as we returned to the cabin, I wasn't sure whether I was glad or not.

When we got back to the cabin, everyone was dressed and ready to leave. We loaded onto the van and headed toward Gatlinburg. About twenty minutes later, Mr. Kendall pulled the van into a parking lot at the edge of town and turned off the key. We could see the town ahead and were all about to jump out of the van when Mr. Kendall shouted, "Hold on now, everybody."

While he spoke, I leaned forward on the edge of my seat and drummed my fingers on the back of the seat in front of me. "Okay now, I don't want anybody going anywhere by themselves," he said. "So everybody find a buddy and stay with that person all day. Remember that we're representing the church." He looked at me. "Everyone be back here no later than five o'clock."

When he finished, we all split up. Me and Walter spent most of the day bumming around in little shops while Walter looked for a Christmas present for his mother. I already had a plan for what I was going to give my mother; it wasn't something I could buy, but it was something I knew she wanted real bad ever since those kids came back from Camp Linden last summer.

I finally talked Walter into going into an arcade. He looked nervous at first and complained that it was a waste of money, but we spent about an hour playing pool. It wasn't much fun because I beat him every game and he treated every shot like a geometry problem.

After we left the arcade, he finally found something for his mother in a glass-blowing shop; it was a clear star. "What would she want with a star?" I asked.

"She'll put it on top of the Christmas tree next year," he answered. "I thought I'd get something in keeping with the season."

"You could buy her two big boxes of candy for what that costs," I said.

"I wonder how far the wise men would have gotten with an almond cluster for a guide." He laughed at his own joke. I didn't; it must have been an honors student thing. So a star had led the wise men to Jesus; it still didn't seem like much of a Christmas present.

Finally, we went into a fancy little ice cream shop. We sat in these swivel chairs that had backs made of black metal in curly patterns. "What kind of ice cream do you want?" Walter asked.

"Chocolate," I answered.

"I'll order," he said. "You have to know how to talk to people in places like this."

When the waitress came to the table, Walter said, "I'll have two scoops of Bordeaux Cherry, and my friend will have two scoops of chocolate." I figured I could've said the same thing.

We sat there the rest of the afternoon, talking about how things was back in middle school. We talked about the sixteen-mile canoe trip we made when it turned cold and started raining about an hour after we started. Me and Walter was the only ones who didn't tip our canoe over that day. We talked about winning the church league basketball tournament. I was the big rebounder; he was the point guard.

Then we didn't talk about nothing. We just sat and watched all the people walking past on the sidewalk. I felt like we was best friends again. I wanted us to be, but I didn't know how to bring it up without sounding dumb. And I knowed things would be different when we got back to school on

Monday. When we got up to go, Walter left fifty cents on the table. I picked it up for him and gave it to him when we was outside. I don't know why, but he smiled sort of funny and said, "Thanks."

When we met back at the van at five o'clock, Walter looked like he wanted to tell somebody something but couldn't. As we rode back, I stared out the window. The sun had just set, and it was getting darker and colder. We were getting close to the cabin, but I was in no hurry. I felt like the weekend was flying by without giving me the chance to do what I wanted to do. I wanted everything to stop for awhile and give me the chance to think things out and find the right words to say.

After supper, while Walter washed dishes, I stepped out onto the deck. I just stood and stared at the stars through the bare trees. I thought about the star Walter had bought earlier in the day and how the star had led the wise men to Jesus. The stars I saw didn't mean nothing, but I figured I could get there just the same. Mr. Kendall opened the sliding glass door and said, "Eddie, is that you?"

"Yep. Yes Sir."

"I thought so. Better come inside. We're about to have evening devotional."

I followed him back inside. We turned out the lights, and everyone sat around the fireplace, talking about the day's events. The flames lit up our faces and made us feel warm and comfortable. It was a good place to be. Finally, Mr. Kendall led the devotion, reading from the Bible about how everybody in the church is a different part of the same body.

"I bet Steve's the stomach," one kid said.

"Well then, you're the nose," Steve answered.

I quit listening and just looked around at everybody. They all seemed so happy and sure of themselves. I knew I wasn't. They all had something important in common; they were like a body, and I was a ragged jacket they threw away. I knew I needed to become a part of their body. Those were the words I was looking for. Finally, Mr. Kendall led a closing prayer. Then everyone ran downstairs, leaving me and Mr. Kendall alone.

I went around picking up the Bibles the others had left scattered all over the floor. Really, I was just keeping busy to put off what I knew I had to do. Finally, I made up my mind. I was going downstairs and tell Walter that I wanted to be a part of their body. I wanted to do it, but I still walked down the stairs real slow. I imagined I was walking the aisle at church. My momma was smiling, and everyone around me was singing:

> *Just as I am, without one plea,*
> *But that thy blood was shed for me,*
> *And that thou bidd'st me come to thee,*
> *O Lamb of God, I come. I come.*

When I got to the bottom of the stairs, I stood there for a minute, about to knock on the door. I could hear Walter talking inside. "I was tired of him following me around on the street in front of all of those people, so I took him into this nice little ice cream shop, in spite of the way he looked," he said. "I ordered for him so he wouldn't sound like a retard. When we got up, I left a tip, and he picked it up and gave it to me when we were outside. It was the dumbest thing I've ever seen."

I did not knock on the door. I walked slowly back up the stairs, trying to be as quiet as possible. The singing was gone, and I could hear everyone laughing downstairs. It made me feel dirty all over. When I got upstairs, I went to the coat rack and grabbed my jacket. I went outside and throwed it as hard as I could over the rail. It got caught on a tree limb and swung like a ghost while I stood in the dark, shaking.

STUART HARRIS was born in Alabama and moved to Tennessee when he was six. He teaches high school in Nashville, and writes from 8 a.m. to noon when not teaching. His poetry has appeared in *West Branch, The Panhandler, The Sucarnochee Review,* and *The Archer.*

Elizabeth Howard

Earthworks

At the Civil War earthworks
on Cumberland Gap,
soldiers waited weary months
for "the battle that never came."
Even now, the black cannon
waits, its hungry mouth pointed
toward an invisible enemy.
The colors of war—bronze,
gold, scarlet, and purple—
abound (hickory, ragweed,
sourwood, asters), but the earth
has worked its magic. An ant
brigade marches in and out
of the cannon's mouth, a platoon
of squirrels storms hickories
and oaks, a squadron of bees
strafes the asters, each
seeking fruits of a different battle.
The rattle of arms has given way
to the rustle of autumn leaves,
whispering of peace and plenty.

The Rope Swing

Driving I-40, I see water
sparkling like a green jewel,
and I long to go once again
to the Buffalo River—to race,
claiming turns, to the rope
swing in the giant sycamore,
despite copperheads
and poison ivy; to soar
over the sandbar, screeching,
arms flapping like a heron's
wings, one with sun
and treetops; to let go
at the perfect moment
(too soon—the sandbar,
too late—the tree roots
jutting out from the jagged
bank); to plunge, gasping
and shivering, into the icy
water, amid bluegill,
redeye, bullfrog,
and pop up like a cork
on a rivercane pole,
eager for the next
skirmish with disaster.

ELIZABETH HOWARD lives and writes in Crossville, finding inspiration for her poetry from various locales around Tennessee.

Roy E. Hutton

The Day After Christmas at Buzzard Rock

We pulled our poor wraps tighter and followed Zenith Whaley's unwavering steps through the winter woods, through decaying leaves, past the endless flow of gray saplings and over ruts and gullies that blended the trail with all that was not the trail, until we were surely lost. But he, of course, was not. He had first walked this path as a boy of four, behind his father, then over and over until the map was traced into his limbs. He was enjoying our first time.

This was Greenbrier, raw, untamed, unlike the popular, groomed areas of Great Smoky Mountains National Park that most visitors view from their car windows. Those areas suffer more each year from the growing hordes of admiring families from the nearby towns and far-away cities, who come to love the park in small doses, and from the dwindling dollars from Washington to pay the rangers and keep up the trails. Greenbrier was never improved so it shows few effects of this neglectful betrayal. It has known such betrayal before.

Earlier on this day after Christmas, we had wandered through old cemeteries with leaning tombstones and hand-carved epitaphs, adding and subtracting the numbers, growing quiet at how many infants lay beneath our feet. We had gazed at the tumbling river, which seemed to flow in a direct line from Greenbrier Pinnacle on the horizon. A year before, a friend's car had tumbled off the bluff just below us, rolling over and over and landing upright in the river, demolished, but leaving him miraculously uninjured. Months before, I hiked alone along a familiar trail at midday. As far as I knew and could see, I was the only human in the area. While scanning the woods beside the trail, my eyes looked into the eyes of a coyote standing proudly on a boulder less than a hundred feet away. We stared at each other, neither daring to move a muscle, for about two minutes. My camera hung by a strap from my neck. I had only inches to bring it to my eye, only one setting to check, so I had to let go with my eyes. When I looked back he was gone, vanished without a sound, challenging me to prove it really happened. I could not prove it to the ranger, who wondered if I had thought to take a picture. It is one of many stories of Greenbrier I have collected, but none have the history and resinous beauty of those Zenith had lived.

He knows all the right moves to make with his eyes, the proper expressions with which to cloak his face, to put at ease all who make his company. He speaks with tone and inflection as he tells him familiar stories, as if he has just recalled that particular experience. He is a teacher, a devout Christian, his gentle strength and power commanding but not intimidating. In his blue overalls and sweat-stained straw fedora, he sets a pace on the trail that takes the wind from hikers half his age. All the while, stories flow like molasses from his lips, unhurried, but as surely moving ahead as anything ever moved. In his younger days he had returned to Greenbrier from down county and manned the firetower, now closed, on Greenbrier Pinnacle, counted fish and studied the pine beetle for the Park Service, and along the way acquired his accidental admirers, those who stumbled upon him hiking the trails, from around the world. We were glad to be within his umbra. He called us his friends.

It had been balmy down below, by the Little Pigeon River, and our light sweaters and flannel had been enough. Now the wind was colder as we climbed higher and higher, pausing as we took staggered resting turns, rapid breaths, exclaiming at the palette of soft colors that falls on the Smokies with winter dusk. For brief moments all of us were still and quiet, then there was no sound but our desperate lungs, and the wind, that not desperate but a soft coo. Away south, beyond the receding folds of mountains and streams, Leconte loomed, its three-peaked silhouette a familiar comfort as the gloaming fell over Greenbrier Cove. Through breaks in the treetops we could see the gravel road below us. A few enthusiasts had parked their cars and taken a marked trail—Ramsay Cascade, Greenbrier Pinnacle, Old Settlers Trail—and did not know we watched them. No one had seen us plunge into the woods behind Zenith, who was sharing a private memory with us. Distracted by his jokes and stories of childhood, by our unsure footing, by the secretness of this path, we did not see Buzzard Rock until it loomed over us, as if it had heard us coming and rose out of the ground to greet us. We were not intruders, Zenith had brought us.

The gray stone erupts from the soft mountainside, massive, a ship's prow marking some eons-gone ocean. It juts skyward, a beacon for birds, who veer toward it from miles away over the Greenbrier. On the maintained trail below from which we had departed, a vast boulder field converges on the gravel path. On either side are church-size chunks of metamorphic rock, gray and brooding, foreboding against the muted winter landscape. They dwarf passing hikers, who wonder whether this might be the day they tumble down from their precarious perches. But, at first sight of the ton upon ton of Buzzard Rock, a rampart unnamed and unmarked on trail maps, I had to reconfigure adjectives for size. Some of the rangers do not know it is here, but old-timers like Zenith, whose childhoods flew by in this cove long before it acquired world-wide lovers, call it their own.

His family had lived in Greenbrier, in the shadow of Buzzard Rock, for four generations before schoolchildren in Tennessee and North Carolina gave pennies and dimes and Rockefeller gave of his fortune to create Great Smoky Mountains National Park. Down below, just as we left the marked trail, Zenith had shown us the boulder his mother had dried peaches and apples in the summer sun, where as an eight-year old he had snitched the sweet treats and darted into the woods. And of course his mamma knew. We walked and climbed on, indifferent to fatigue, while he told of his boyhood fear of RiverMan, his pranks with his cousins, his love for his father and how much he missed his counsel.

We came upon the old homesite of Uncle Pinckney Whaley, so Zenith called him, who had built a new log home close to a spring, gone up higher to dig ramps to transplant close to the house and water source. Pinckney did not know that, in only one more year, strangers would come and tell him his bleak choices, both meaning that he must move on. Pinckney had built a fence of locust posts to keep in his stock, and the graying remnants stand still with rusty nails. No man can pull them out now. They wait. An old cookstove lies broken on stones that had been the chimney, and there is for certain no family here now. With a gentle prod of his stick, Zenith uncovered the tender ramp shoots that would sprout in a few weeks, as they had for decades, where his uncle had put them.

When the park was formed, hundreds of families sadly gave up the small farms that had passed down to them from fathers and grandfathers, received a few dollars per acre, and moved away. Some turned their backs from the mountains and departed for the cities of Knoxville or Chattanooga; others slipped across the road and up a nearby hollow, to watch from a few miles away their beloved mountains pass the seasons. The grandeur of this park, so cherished by its friends who return year after year to walk its woods, was bought for us all by the sorrow of the families who had to say goodbye.

Before them, of course, were the Cherokee, but that is a longer, even sadder story. Buzzard Rock had been witness to it all, its story longer than any of us could know, the four of us hiking to plumb some history from this anonymous national park. Oh, it may have settled some fraction of an inch further into the rich soil — of course the rain and wind had worn away some gneiss and rounded its specks of white quartz, but no one had been there to witness. And the rock is silent.

The four of us climbed upon it. Zenith led the way, his feet sure and familiar with the steeply sloping surface. We gamely followed, laughing because there were no words for this moment. One of us climbed down and snapped a photo, the rest sitting like specks atop buzzard Rock, fifty feet from the ground, smiling at our good fortune.

We climbed down as darkness approached, circled the base of the rock, and made our way down to the road. Two buzzards swooped in from their carrion hunt, rested briefly, then circled away over Greenbrier Cove.

Enjoyed your reading so much

Roy E Hutton

ROY E. HUTTON is a native middle Tennessean, with a Ph.D. from Peabody College of Vanderbilt. He makes his living as a clinical psychologist in Nashville, listening to the stories of others.

Susie Sims Irvin

Always Before This Summer

I do not hear a call to the podium.
I am not the poet of this summer.

I sing of tall dark corn
filled out and tasseled
crowding single file into chosen fields,
of succulent stems that snap
and generous pastureland
rolled up in great round bales,
of lazy laughing summers meandering
to nowhere in particular.

I am not the bard
of this imposter
who fries our days
and tosses them one upon another
cow chips
stacked in the hot metal bed of a pick-up,
who squeezes from the creases of night
that last hoping and leaves it limp
wrung out
sentencing its creatures
to empty wandering searches
in scrawny coats of castigated indignity.

I find no voice
for an impotent earth staring crazed
into the white heat of a nothing sky
teeth clinched in protracted agony
beneath stubble singed to final brown.

Best wishes
Susie Sims Irvin

I strain instead
with the red rimmed eyes of the farmer
who abandons his tractor in mid field
succumbing to swirling dust fine as face powder
death mask of the vanishing topsoil
that he has nurtured with his days and nights
held to his breast spewed with his sweat
and now drips with dry white tears
of surrender.

How much do I hear for one ordinary neighbor?
What will you give me for
his pride, his youth, his dream,
watered in one lifelong crap game
gambling that it would rain eventually
because it always had before?
Always before this summer.

SUSIE SIMS IRVIN grew up on a family farm in Williamson County, near Franklin. She is the author of two self-published volumes, *Shhh... It's time for the devotional*, and *Falls Even Now the Seed*.

Marilyn Kallet

After Your Visit

(For Robert Hass)

Oh Bob, the voices that still live within us!
Rounding the curve at Blueridge,
it's 1968. I'm twenty.
My lover Tom Barefoot (yes!)
tells his mother, "you know what I hate most
about Marilyn? Her bourgeois morality!"
"I know," she responds.
I'm napping upstairs, but their voices carry
through an air vent.
Ten years later, his letter:
"I have a daughter now.
Her name is Honey in Sanskrit.
My anger against you has finally lifted."
Ten years more, I've lost his address..
I respond: "Dear Tom,
I too have a daughter. Being a mother
is a long process of healing. It's better now
than when we were together in one body."

Do present actions influence the past?
Can our words survive the sharp turns back?
Your poems return me to "small songs,"
"glistening wet wood."
Red Flame and Iceberg roses surround our house this May.
Heather skips across the grass, the grey cat in her arms.
"Mama, did you write a poem yet about the blue heron?"
Late afternoon, rounding the curve on Blueridge
I slow the car, Heather scans the reservoir
for our alphabet of birds.

Why Not Blossom Instead?
The natural world is a spiritual house—

intimate as skin, made of
dawn, evening light, purple stars,
invisible poets whose voices reach me
through tiny petalled mikes.
I'm speaking within William Stafford again.

He says what I need to hear: "It's okay
that you didn't win the poetry Series—
                                        why hang your ego
on that hook? Why not blossom lightly
from a pink dogwood?" Dutifully
I protest that I'm Jewish,
the dogwood is linked to the story of Christ.

"Trees are non-denominational,"
he laughs. He's as real to me as this
bed of wildflowers, this late sun pale and warm,
a goblet of apricot liqueur.

A river of violets answers when I look for
                                        more of him.
I turn to the flowers for advice
an old friend might have offered.
An unusual animal chirps from the grass:
                        "So, your husband wanted this
victory for you? Whisper the truth
over him. Make corsages
of it, make forests filled with mutual sprays
                                        of untamed blooms.
Call the wildest orchid Losing."

MARILYN KALLET is Professor of English and Director of the
Creative Writing Program at the University of Tennessee at
Knoxville. She is author of five books, and a founder of the TWA.

Helga K. Kidder

Friday Night Lyrics

We were acting on a whim, a fancy,
wanting to step into a chic bar
the paper called *Clearwater Cafe*
conjuring images of a trout-filled
fresh-water stream, were met in front
by an American cowboy. *Better go
in here*, he pointed at the side door
opening to the band's jazz guitars and
Baby-why-is-your-bacon-fat blues,
jeans, T-shirt families, rocking,
short-jeaned girls itching in bar stools,
I dressed to the Nines for eating out fancy,
yes, and now in a beer joint or so
it seems, we swill beer, frothing beer from
bottles on dried, middle-aged throats,
one, two, three for you, I stop,
the guitars rock — we were going to have
a fine dinner, bouillabaisse perhaps
or fresh trout cakes in tomato coulis,
vintage chardonnay — but the guitars vibrate,
unsettle smoke, voices, beside us a
blonde-braided two-year-old in a red and white
polka-dot dirndl, swinging her small fists
with throbbing guitars, coarse lyrics,
blue eyes, mouth in perfect OOo's, yes,
like that and I'm new, too, when you,
you slip, yes, your hand in mine, and no,
we hadn't done this in a long time.

In Media Res: A Damsel in Distress

This is not a picnic.
It is discovery of a missing shingle
that unsettles the entire roof
under a threatening sky.
I lie with my mouth wide open.
A pair in face masks lean over me.
They examine the roof
of my mouth & the great room
of great words on my tongue & between
my teeth. Why do they answer
their questions with the drill's shrill
whine while I try to walk
through the maze of leafless branches
outside the picture window? All the while,
my silent song resonates
in the tightly woven baskets hanging
from hooks & the wallpaper's gridwork.
And an army of ants have begun marching
on my tongue. I wonder if language advanced
slowly from our throats or if it broke free
like an avalanche of stones the moment
we stopped climbing trees, stopped
regurgitating leaves. I want to bite
the pair's hands or at least chew
chips, sip wine on a houndstooth
throw, raise my nose toward the bright,
warming rays. The woman insists
I stay with my teeth
dipped in soft clay to set my bite.
I keep my legs crossed at the ankles
at least til behind me the man sounds
a chime, a bell announcing lunch
or perhaps the arrival of spring.
Now I will spring

from the chair, begin again,
multilingual
with a stutter, a phrase
like these buds dotting branches,
soon breaking free
a universal tale.

HELGA K. KIDDER is a native of Germany's Black Forest, but has lived in Tennessee since 1965. In addition to her own writing, she translates contemporary German poets, and has a translation chapbook, *Gravel*. Kidder currently resides in Chattanooga.

For a fellow writer
Carol Luther

Carol Luther

Burying Edna

The battle for the cemetery lot began as a simple skirmish. Aunt Violet called Mama, an experienced non-combatant. Violet warned Mama, since my daddy Everett was out, that Aunt Pet was going to call and that she wanted to talk to Everett after Pet called. After discussing what a trial and tribulation her two girls were because they never paid enough attention to her, she said good-bye. Mama hung up, "What now, Jan?"

My aunts had fought a stubborn war for my father's soul. Being the only boy among six sisters, he was always pressured to take sides in their quarrels. Their shifting alliances would dismay a seasoned diplomat.

Mama maintained neutrality with a sense of humor. I classified myself a journalistic observer.

I witnessed these events while I waited for job interviews to pour in from my multitudinous applications to school systems and newspapers (B.A. in History and Journalism). I had something to "fall back on" with my teaching certificate, but it was beginning to look as if what I was going to fall back on was my parents' hospitality.

My father, in general, had as little to do with my aunts as possible, having learned long ago that you could not please one without displeasing another.

The Sisters were Rose, Petunia (Pet), Violet, Iris, Magnolia (Maggie), and Daisy. I knew them and their husbands reasonably well, but the cousins, in-laws, and other assorted relations remained fuzzy in my mind. I don't mean to be vague about my cousins, but because my father was next to youngest, and he and Mama had me after they were both thirty, most of my cousins were quite a bit older than I was. I had little contact with them except at funerals or weddings because of my father's aloofness. He wished to show no favoritism.

Anyway, The Sisters vexed him. Poor Daddy, for having been raised with six sisters, he didn't understand women very well. Or maybe he did.

I jumped when the phone rang again, "Pet," Mama predicted, bravely answering.

"Oh, Effie, hello," Mama said cordially. Cousin Effie Watkins lived with her mother Pet Watkins and played secretary because Pet's eyesight caused her trouble in dialing the phone. Effie, unlike her five siblings, had never left home, and the main business of her life was her mother's business. A person can be pushier and more obstinate about someone else's business than she can be about her own because she doesn't have to worry about being delicate.

Effie announced that she was bringing Aunt Pet to see Daddy on her way home from Pet's appointment with the eye doctor.

After Mama hung up, she and I looked at each other. "Wonder what?" I said. Mama sighed.

I missed The Visit, but Mama and Daddy summarized the vital points at supper. Daddy was exasperated.

"It's about Mam and Pap's cemetery plot," Mama began. Mam and Pap, Daddy's parents, were buried at Tarriffville Community Methodist Church in Sequoyah County, forty miles away from where Mama and Daddy had lived all their adult lives in Craigsfort. Next to Mam and Pap's resting place was room for two other burials in the family plot. I'd never contemplated who might have the honor of being buried their.

"Effie wants to know if they can bury her sister Edna next to Mam and Pap," Mama continued.

"When did she die?" I asked.

"She's not dead," Daddy said.

"Is she sick?"

"No," Mama said. "As best I could get it, her husband's gone off with some other woman. Edna's going to leave Atlanta and come live with Pet and Effie."

"But why are they worrying about where to bury her? How old is she?" I asked, having never met her.

Mama calculated. "She must be around 59 or 60."

"Good gracious, she could live twenty years or more! Why are they trying to bury her?"

Mama shrugged, "I think she's had a nervous breakdown or something. She's real depressed."

"You mean she might kill herself? I think if my family were looking for a place to bury me that it might make me a little glum to."

"That old Ralph, her husband, he's done this twice before. She'll be back with him just like the other times," my father said dismissively.

"But Pet said he was going to divorce Edna this time," Mama reminded him.

"Ralph's said that before too. And so has she."

Daddy didn't believe in nervous breakdowns or depressions. He always thought a person just needed to get a hold of himself.

The phone rang. Mama and I looked at Daddy, "It's for you," she said. Daddy hated answering the phone.

He picked it up.

"Hello.... Yes.... Yes... This afternoon.... Really?.... I'm thinking about it."

Mama and I twisted with impatience. Daddy's noncommittal phone conversations were cryptic.

"Rose," Mama guessed.

"Maggie," I speculated.

Daddy finally hung up. "That was Iris. She sounded like she was jumping up off the floor." I pictured my seventy year-old aunt hopping up and down in a fit of pique like Rumpelstiltskin. "She told me not to let Pet bury Edna in Mam and Pap's grave. Oh, she was letting fly on Pet." He laughed.

"What *did* you tell Aunt Pet and Effie about burying Edna there?" I asked.

Daddy seemed surprised that I would even ask. "Why, they don't need that plot now."

Mama and I looked at each other. When my father made a Pronouncement, that was that, and no power on earth would make him change once it was pronounced, as I had discovered in earlier years. Tears, tantrums, whining, and sulking had no effect on him when I wanted to do something that he pronounced as unnecessary.

Aunt Rose, the eldest, who was the widow of an insurance agent, called soon after the pronouncement. Daddy's end of the conversation was opaque. "I didn't....I haven't...I won't....I wasn't....Umm....That's nice....A Taurus?....Well, bye." Rose saw no need to give anybody a cemetery plot at the moment. Also, she was buying one of her daughters a car so that she wouldn't move to California.

Aunt Maggie and Uncle Vern came that evening to discuss the situation with Daddy, interrupting him in his yard work.

Maggie opined, in her whispery drawl, that there was nothing wrong with Edna. She didn't think that Edna even wanted to come up here. Her theory was that the whole thing was Pet's and Effie's idea. "It's because Effie has always wanted that spot next to Mam because she says Mam raised her, Everett, which is true because that's when Pet got sick for such a long time. Effie was the stubbornest baby you ever saw and like to drove Mam crazy. Wouldn't sleep. Wouldn't eat. Always had to be held."

I asked if Edna had a job.

Mama thought that she had taught school for a little while, but not in years.

Maggie nodded and said that Edna had lasted for a few weeks until a little boy climbed a tree and wouldn't come down. Edna burst into tears and said she wasn't hired to climb a tree, so she went back to her classroom and put on her hat and resigned that minute. "Of course, she couldn't have gotten a teaching job after that if she'd wanted to," Maggie laughed.

Mama, who herself had tried teaching and disliked it, agreed that teaching was stressful.

Edna had married Ralph soon after the tree climbing.

Ralph, Daddy allowed, was nothing but a drunk. He pronounced that as if that described Ralph's character for all time as well as Edna's for having had the bag judgment to marry him in the first place. Daddy didn't hold with the idea that alcoholism was a disease.

Maggie agreed and admitted that while, of course, she didn't believe in divorce, she thought that Edna was better off without Ralph, and she didn't understand why Edna was so upset this time in particular since separating was almost a habit with her and Ralph.

Vern put in his nickel's worth by pointing out that Edna had those three children who could be taking care of her, so Pet and Effie didn't need to bring her all the way up here from Atlanta.

So three of the six sisters, Rose, Maggie, and Iris, had committed themselves to Daddy's side.

After Maggie and Vern left, Daddy fell asleep on the couch, exhausted by the unanimity shown thus far by his heretofore contentious sisters. Mama and I continued our conversation.

"Now let me get this straight—Daddy decides who can be buried there. Could he be buried there?"

"Umm-hmm. Mam and Pap left it for Daddy to decide after they died."

"Do you want to be buried there with Daddy?"

"Oh, no, I couldn't be buried there!"

"Why not?"

"Oh, law, his sisters wouldn't let me be buried there! I'm not one of the children."

"But you've been married to Daddy for thirty years. He wouldn't want to be buried without you!"

"Well, I guess not..." Mama shrugged and laughed.

"So there's room for two people next to Mam and Pap and nobody but their children can use it, no husbands or wives need apply."

"That's about it."

"If Daddy were buried there, could I be buried there? I mean, if he has the say so, shouldn't I be able to be buried there?" My final resting place began to assume some importance. After all, we know not what tomorrow may bring.

Mama cautiously said that if I died first, it might be all right, but if I died after Daddy did, the aunts wouldn't abide it. Evidently primogeniture and the Code of Hammurabi (though Mama didn't use those terms) had something to do with inheriting. I could foresee a complex legal case evolving if I wanted to make a claim. Would a jury take pity on my status as an only child?

What if I got married? Could my husband be buried in the family plot? I was getting too far ahead. First, I had to die before Daddy did so that Daddy could establish my claim. I was irked. This was complicated.

I occurred to me that perhaps I should consult a lawyer. Or a funeral home.

Also, I gloomily recollected, I still didn't have a job. But then, if I died tomorrow, why would I need a job?

The next day the other sisters checked in.

Aunt Violet called while Daddy was washing the car to let us know that she was sitting there in that big old house all by herself.

Violet said that nobody ever told her anything. Billie Jo and Thelma were so busy with work that she didn't get to see them much, and she didn't want to drive all the way to Knoxville by herself to see them. That was just too much traffic for a senior citizen like her.

Mama agreed that traffic was just awful.

Violet instructed Mama to tell Daddy not to let Effie and those other Watkinses have that plot. Also, Daddy should call Daisy and see what she thought. And tell him to come see her (Violet) when he was in the neighborhood, because she didn't get much company. Folks just didn't visit the way they used to. They stayed home and watched TV.

Mama promised to pass on Violet's strictures.

In addition to the disruption caused by having five sisters and Effie calling frequently, the times they called were inconvenient, like just before Daddy left for work or right as we sat down to eat.

Iris called at lunch to reiterate her support for Daddy's decision. She also reported on her sainted son, her angelic daughter-in-law, and her cherubic grandchildren. She had omitted those details in her previous call, which showed how incensed she was. Daddy listened with noncommittal "umm's" as the green beans cooled in his plate.

It was a phenomenon. The Sisters, who were usually split into two or three factions, were solidly behind Daddy. Furthermore, their considerable firepower was all ranged against the same object. It should have given Pet and Effie pause, but they, or at least Effie, charged blindly ahead.

Daddy did not know what to make of The Sisters' agreement. He had spent most of his adult life trying to remain remote from their internecine wars, and now he found himself surrounded by their support as he opposed one of them. It made him nervous and irritable.

My nerves were unraveling too. I was convinced that I was missing calls for interviews because of the aunts tying up the phone.

The next morning Mama reminded Daddy that Violet had suggested that he call Daisy.

"What difference does it make to her? Daisy's not coming back here to be buried! Did you salt these eggs? It doesn't taste like it!"

It took three days for Effie to phone all the aunts to try to change their minds, with no success. Some of the aunts might have been swayed individually, but with General Everett taking command, they were entrenched. So Effie was forced to call the general to negotiate.

Daddy was not happy when he answered the phone. Effie talked loudly enough for me to hear across the room as I sat reading the newspaper, reduced to searching the classifieds. Effie informed him that her mama was just crying her eyes out.

"Oh," Daddy said.

Pet was so worried because Edna wasn't any better., Effie told him. Down in Atlanta, Edna was crying her eyes out too.

"Ummm."

She was just crying and crying and she wouldn't leave the house.

"Pet?"

Yes and Edna too, both of them were crying their eyes out, Effie said. She would feel better if she knew that she had a final resting place.

Daddy asked if it was <u>Edna</u> that would feel better if she knew she had a final resting place.

No, her <u>Mama</u> would feel better, Effie explained. She had been so torn up about Ralph and Edna. But it might help Edna too.

Daddy asked her if she meant that Edna would quit crying if she knew she had a cemetery plot up here.

Effie definitely thought so.

Daddy said that maybe Edna would get back together with Ralph because she had twice before, so there didn't seem to be any hurry.

"Ummm," said Effie.

Our discussion at lunch was illuminating. Daddy slapped the mashed potatoes into his plate. "Edna doesn't know a thing about this. This is all Effie and Pet's idea to get that lot because Effie wants to be buried by Mam. Well, she's not going to get it."

I interposed a question. "But don't the Watkinses have a plot of their own—"

"Right at the foot of Mam and Pap's, crowding right in there practically touching. But they won't stop until they have that other part too. Effie said she wanted to be next to Mam because Mam practically raised her. Well, she ain't going to be resting there next to Mam. Pet and Effie and that crowd of Watkinses caused Mam enough trouble when she was alive, and they're not going to be worrying her now. There's no salt in these potatoes."

Mama passed the salt.

He wasn't finished. "Pet was always leaving Earl and going home to stay for a while or sending the kids there for Mam to look after. Now Earl had his good points, but he sure could be a trial, and I'll tell you so could Pet. I'd say they were about even in meanness. She needs to tell Edna to get on with things. It's not doing her one bit of good to sit there and cry. I believe this meat needs to be cooked a little more."

"What Edna needs is a job," I said.

The aunts continued to check in. Daisy, who lived in Michigan and whom I'd seen only once, at my grandfather's funeral, called for clarification. She talked to Mama, for naturally Daddy was away, at the bank, when she called. She was bemused by all the furor.

"You tell him to do what he wants," Daisy said as she hung up. "Donnie and I already have a lot here."

Mama turned to me. "I wish I didn't have to be the answering machine."

The aunts escalated their show of solidarity. They invited Daddy over for supper or lunch or a visit. Daddy declined all the invitations. "If I go to one of them, I'd have to go to all of them, so I'm not going to any of them," he said in fraying tones at supper. "Where's the biscuits? I thought you said we were having biscuits!"

Then came a strange lull with nothing more heard from Pet or Effie for a few days. Rumors flew. Edna had a nervous breakdown and was in a mental institution. Effie went to Atlanta and had Ralph arrested for taking some of Edna's money. Ralph had Effie arrested for threatening him. Edna tried to shoot Ralph. Ralph tried to shoot Edna.

Mama and I waited, anticipating sensational events, but none occurred. Instead, like some inevitable law of physics, Ralph returned to Edna, and she took him back. Personally, I was disappointed. Iris had the pleasure of telling us how things had transpired with Edna, and that her son (Iris's) had received a promotion.

Pet and Effie never did tell Daddy that they no longer needed the cemetery lot. The last I know of Effie and the cemetery is that one of the church deacons caught her taking flowers off all the graves the day after Mother's Day.

Mama and Daddy looked at a lot in the Craigsfort City Cemetery later that summer.

And on a hot August day as I prepared my classroom for the first day of my ninth graders, I decided to be cremated.

But I'm going to keep that a secret. If Effie finds out, she'll do it first—and have her ashes sprinkled on Mam's grave.

CAROL LUTHER is a native of Maryville, and teaches composition and literature at Pellissippi State Technical Community College in Knoxville. She hopes to write fiction that portrays a distinctive east Tennessee culture and outlook.

Bedford Hamilton McCoin

Homer's First Case

Elizabeth,
thanks for asking

Mac

Homer kept the tape rolling as Herbert Donnelly and Elisa Hartman embraced by the side of Elisa's Honda Civic. When the shotgun blasts rang out, Homer thought a truck was backfiring repetitively. But when the couple crumpled to the ground, he knew his first case had become complicated beyond his wildest dreams.

On a chilly October Monday morning, two days previous, Homer Paine had sat in his new one-room office, Reeboks propped on his new used desk, in the second week of his new career, reading an old textbook on forensic medicine and wondering if the phone would ever ring. Obligingly enough, at that moment it did. Homer's feet hit the floor and he grabbed for the receiver.

"Homer Paine, Private Investigator."

"Homer," a familiar voice said, "do you own a camera?"

"Yes, sir, Mr. Crafton," Homer replied, visualizing his dapper former boss on the other end of the line. "I have an old camcorder in the closet."

"That will do nicely. I have a job for you—if your moral sense can handle it."

Homer's cheeks grew warm despite his elation at the thought of getting his first case. "Yes, sir. I mean, I think I can. What's the job?"

"We need pictures of a man and his girlfriend."

Homer's embarrassment became more acute. "Sir, I won't do motel rooms."

"Nothing like that. Just shots of them together, being

160

affectionate, you know."

His voice brightened. "In that case, my fee is $200 a day and expenses."

Crafton chuckled. "You made that much when you worked with us, five days a week guaranteed."

"Yes, sir, I know."

"You could still come back."

"Sorry, Mr. Crafton. I can't do that."

"I see. Well, the man's name is Herbert Donnelly."

"Donnelly the architect?"

"Yes. I don't suppose you have a fax, so I'll send you his file by special messenger. We don't know the woman. That's your job."

"When do you need the pictures?"

Another chuckle: "Yesterday."

Taking the back stairs two at a time, Homer ducked through the door leading to the parking lot where he kept his '83 Olds. A hand-me-down from his father, the old car fit his 6'4" frame and got him where he wanted to go.

He drove to his condo apartment wondering if he should reconsider Mr. Crafton's offer. At age twenty-five, he was a neophyte in a tough business, but he was used to challenges. They had called him "The Stork" when he first went out for basketball at West High in Nashville, but he'd gone on a weight-building program and eventually made all-city as the team's starting forward. When his classmates called him "Mr. Smith" in college, as much for his resemblance to Jimmy Stewart in the old movie, *Mr. Smith Goes to Washington*, as for his impassioned pleas on behalf of justice in the mock trials at law school, he took pride in the name and became even more ardent in defense of justice. Ultimately his moral sense had cost him his law career—well, almost, he thought.

Homer's condo, legacy of legal-intern days, on which he now hoped just to keep up the payments, was one of twenty condo apartments in a converted warehouse on State Street near Old City. The camcorder rested on a closet shelf. To his surprise, it still worked. His parents had given him the camera as a basketball practice aid. He had put it away in '88 when, at his father's insistence, he agreed to attend law school instead of accepting a basketball scholarship at Austin Peay.

He had gone to the University of Tennessee law school in Knoxville instead of Vanderbilt, for he wanted to be sure any success he achieved would be because of his own efforts, not those of his father and grandfather before him.

With camcorder in the trunk, Homer returned to his office. A manila envelope lay on his desk, apparently put there by the building's gray-haired receptionist and secretary-for-hire. For the next thirty minutes, he pored over the Herbert Donnelly file.

Donnelly's architectural firm specialized in shopping malls. Donnelly and his wife, Gloria, were both ardent sportspersons. An old newspaper photograph showed them grouse hunting in Scotland. Their names turned up regularly in the society columns of the News-Sentinel. They were about to make the news section as well, Homer surmised. Herbert Donnelly was fooling around and Gloria Donnelly knew it. Homer's job was to get the evidence.

He studied a recent photo of Donnelly and his wife. Neither looked the part. Herbert's lined face and mane of silvery hair made him appear older than his fifty-two years, while Gloria's sharp features and dark hair bunned tightly in back reminded Homer of somebody's old maid aunt. Trouble must have been brewing when the picture was taken, for Gloria's dark eyes seemed haunted by pain.

Since it would be his first surveillance, Homer gave himself plenty of time. At 4:00 Monday afternoon, he parked behind the Donnelly building and put his last two quarters in a parking meter. After a short search of the building's parking garage, he discovered a late-model, dark green Jaguar parked next to the elevator with Donnelly's name stenciled on the concrete-block wall behind it.

Homer returned to his own car, checked the meter, and saw it would soon expire. He jogged up Union to Gay Street and got change at a MacDonald's. While there, he bought two cheeseburgers and a coke to go.

Donnelly's Jaguar was still in its slot when Homer returned, and Homer settled down to wait in his own car. After changing positions a dozen times, he began to wonder about his career choice.

He knew his real reason for bucking his father's wishes and making his mother question his basic intelligence involved more than what he had told Mr. Crafton. He had read suspense novels from the time he was a teenager, and an on-going fascination with fictional heroes such as Sam Spade, Perry Mason, and Travis McGee had probably affected his decision as well. Being assigned by Mr. Crafton to defend a known criminal had been the last straw in his legal career, but Homer knew it wasn't the only straw.

At 5:00, a Honda Civic pulled to the curb near Homer's car on the nearly-deserted back street. A few moments later, a man Homer readily identified as Herbert Donnelly walked up the garage ramp and over to the Honda. Homer turned on the camcorder and began taping through the windshield. He despaired of getting a clear shot until, at the last minute, the car door opened and an attractive, busty blonde in her thirties reached up to give Donnelly a good-bye kiss and hug. As she drove away, Donnelly returned to the garage. Seconds later his green Jaguar zoomed up the ramp.

Homer followed. He caught a light on West Cumberland and almost lost the sports car, but when it turned off Kingston Pike onto Cherokee Boulevard, he knew Donnelly was on his way home.

Homer staked out Donnelly's lakeview residence. He wondered about the blonde, contenting himself with the thought that if the camcorder tape wasn't clear enough, he at least had her license number. He counted joggers until darkness came. He ate cold cheeseburgers and drank warm coke. Later he relieved himself in a clump of bushes, hoping night joggers wouldn't notice. He listened to a talk show on the car radio. When the downstairs lights in Donnelly's house went out at ten p.m., he called it a night.

Back at his condo, Homer ran the camcorder tape. Though the blonde's face was visible in profile, he decided it might not be enough for a jury.

The next morning he drove to the City-County Building, identified himself to a clerk in Vehicle Registration, and gave her the license-plate number. A computer supplied a name, Elisa Hartman, and a north Knoxville address. The phone book listed a Carl Hartman at the same address.

After lunch Homer returned to his office and called Mr. Crafton. After a quick summary of what he had done so far, he asked his former mentor if he could find out about a Carl Hartman and his wife. Crafton said he would check with a friend in city administration and get back.

An hour later a Crafton legal intern called Homer. Carl Hartman was a former construction worker for TVA who had lost his job in a recent cutback. Elisa Hartman taught English, art, and music at Bearden Elementary School in west Knoxville. According to school records, she had tutored a Donnelly granddaughter at their residence this past summer.

Homer was surprised Gloria Donnelly had let the voluptuous Elisa Hartman within a mile of her husband, and even more surprised she would divorce him over the affair. Of course if he came up with the evidence, Gloria Donnelly could afford her choice of new husbands.

He drove to Bearden Elementary School and parked at the curb where he had a view of the front entrance. While keeping one eye on the school, he skimmed a back issue of "American Handgunner." He thought about the foxy redhead in his forensic medicine adult education class and wondered if she would like to go with him to the rifle range.

At three o'clock children erupted from the building.

Homer sat up, camcorder at the ready. A half-hour later Elisa Hartman hadn't appeared. With sinking spirits, he realized she'd probably parked at the back of the school.

For variety he bought dinner to go from a Burger King. This time he used the restroom and made sure he had plenty of quarters. He drove to the rear of the Donnelly Building, deposited quarters in the meter, and waited.

At 5:30, Donnelly's Jaguar appeared. Homer followed to the City-County building, then watched in dismay as the car disappeared into an underground parking garage. He found a space a half block away, filled the meter, and scrunched down in the seat to wait. He wondered what had made him think P.I. work was exciting.

He thought about his former girlfriend Denise who had gotten tired of waiting and married a CPA. He missed Denise, though not enough to marry her even if she were still available. He listened to the radio.

Three hours later, Donnelly's car roared out of the City-County garage. Homer again followed. Again he waited until the lights went out at Donnelly's lakeside residence before returning to his condo.

On Wednesday morning Homer wrote a long-hand report to Mr. Crafton summarizing his activities on the case. He dropped off the report and the tape at Crafton's building and went to the YMCA for an hour's workout. Afterward, he picked up a box of business cards ordered the week before from an office-supply store. While there, he priced faxes and found they were indeed out of his price range. Back in the office after a hotdog lunch, he wrote a letter to his parents in Nashville saying he was fine and enclosing his new business card.

At 3:00, he drove again to Bearden Elementary school, parking this time where he could see the rear of the building. About 3:15, Elisa Hartman came out talking gaily, almost flirtatiously, with a tall, slender woman who parted her short brunette hair on the side like a man. They both wore flat-heeled shoes and carried satchels.

Elisa told the woman good-bye and unlocked the door of her Honda. Homer tracked her with the camcorder until she drove away, then followed her car to a small house in north Knoxville. As Elisa pulled into the driveway, Homer glided to the curb two houses away. He slumped down and aimed the camera out the open driver's window.

Through the zoom lens he saw a man in a checkered shirt he assumed was Carl Hartman washing a pickup truck in the carport. A single-barreled shotgun hung on a rack in the truck's rear window. When Elisa got out of her car, the lean, wiry-haired man walked over, kissed her on the cheek, and appeared to ask a question. She shook her head and continued into the house. Water puddled at the man's feet as his hand mindlessly squeezed a wet sponge.

At 4:30, Homer parked again at the rear of the Donnelly Building. At 5:00, Donnelly's Jaguar nosed up the ramp.

With Homer trailing, Donnelly drove north on I-75 to Clinton Highway. From there he proceeded north five miles and turned into the gravel parking lot of a roadhouse with a portable sign in front reading, "Barney's Bar and Grill."

Homer pulled into the emergency lane and waited. Donnelly parked near a stand of trees next to what looked like Elisa Hartmann's Honda. He got out, wearing a gray suit and no tie, and walked into the roadhouse. Homer pulled into the lot, positioned the Olds where he would have a clear view of both cars, and followed the architect inside.

An old jukebox played Hank Williams Jr's "All my Rowdy Friends." The half-dozen men at the bar looked up as Homer entered, then refocused on their beer and TV news. Donnelly wasn't among them. Homer ordered a beer and took it into the back room. Only a few couples occupied the tables and booths. One couple swayed in place on a tiny dance floor to Hank's grinding melody.

Homer's eyes adjusted to the dark interior. Donnelly and Elisa Hartman sat side by side in a back booth, sipping beer and talking quietly. They appeared to be holding hands.

166

Homer felt sorry for Donnelly then, though not enough to keep him from doing his job. He remembered the pain in Gloria Donnelly's eyes.

Homer returned to his car, thankful that daylight savings had another week to go. He removed the camcorder from the trunk. Thirty minutes later the door of the roadhouse opened and Donnelly and Hartman walked out arm in arm. Homer let the camera roll. The two strolled to Elisa's car, stopped, and embraced. That's when the shooting began.

Homer kept taping when Donnelly and Elisa Hartman toppled to the ground even though his hands trembled and a hot pulse pounded in his neck. When the firing stopped, Homer lowered the camera, put a shaky hand on the door handle, thought better of it, and leaned on the horn. Seconds later a short, obese man in white shirt and suspenders stuck his head out the front door of the roadhouse and glared angrily in Homer's direction. Homer leaped from the car.

"Over here!" he yelled as he ran toward the fallen couple.

Blood was everywhere. The spray of shotgun pellets had obliterated the victims' faces. A retching sound caused Homer to turn around just in time to witness the fat man, later identified as Barney, throw up. Homer ran to the roadhouse, trying not to be sick himself, and yanked open the door.

"Somebody call the police!" he shouted to the startled beer drinkers.

The police questioned Homer for more than two hours. When they learned why he was at the roadhouse, they impounded his tape and sent cars to pick up Gloria Donnelly and Carl Hartman.

Modern technology being what it is, the police were able to enhance Homer's tape until it produced a clear picture of the perpetrator hidden among the leaves at the edge of the parking. Otherwise they might have arrested Carl Hartman for the crime. This realization made Homer stop questioning his decision to become a P.I.

As for Gloria Donnelly, her computer-enhanced, wild-eyed visage appeared clearly, firing a single-barreled pump shotgun. The strange thing was not Gloria's hatred, but what had brought it about. When the police showed her Homer's tape of the shooting, she broke down and confessed. Elisa had been her target, not Donnelly. Donnelly had been unfaithful too many times for her to kill him over that. The knowledge of his infidelities, however, enabled her to respond with a clear conscience to Elisa's seductive overtures when they had visited, over wine, after the tutoring sessions.

As her love affair with Elisa blossomed, Gloria decided to divorce her husband in hopes she could entice Elisa into getting a divorce and moving in with her. She knew Herbert was seeing someone, and proof of it would sway the settlement her way; but she never dreamed the other woman might be Elisa.

When Gloria saw Homer's pictures of Elisa and Donnelly kissing, she knew Elisa had either fallen for Herbert or was angling for a bigger financial catch. Either way, Gloria felt betrayed and decided to kill them both. She took a pump shotgun from her husband's collection, removed the restrictor plug, and loaded the gun with ten twelve-gauge shells. She staked out Elisa's house just as Homer had, then followed her lover to the roadhouse and waited in the trees for them to come out.

In thinking about the case afterward, Homer decided it had been a losing situation for everyone—the Donnellys, the Hartmans, even Mr. Crafton when the court committed Gloria to a mental institution—everyone except, strangely enough, Homer himself. Mr. Crafton gave him a bonus for the danger he had faced, and Crafton's firm was even now representing him in a bidding war between two TV networks for use of his tape on their live-action police shows. He wouldn't have to worry about mortgage payments for a while.

The next Monday morning Homer sat in his office, Reeboks propped on his new used desk, forensic-medicine textbook in hand, feeling a sense of déja vu. His first case was history, yet he was wondering if his phone would ever ring again. As if on cue, it did.

BEDFORD HAMILTON McCOIN is retired, and therefore, a full-time writer. He has been vigorously writing novels for eighteen months, and makes his home in Knoxville.

Carol Brooks Norris

Porch Peace
Psalms of a Midlife Woman

August 6, 1994

It's about 8:15 and the fog is beginning to lift. Saturday morning on a screened porch in East Tennessee may be as close to complete peace as I'll ever get this side of Heaven. For August, the temperatures have dipped to unusual lows. The air was almost too cool for bringing my breakfast out, but cool is the desirable goal these days when my body regularly makes more heat than necessary.

The early hour plus the fog are responsible for a noticeable lack of human noise; but the birds are talkative, and seasonal insects are providing background music, a humming so familiar that I actually had to concentrate to distinguish it from the hum my brain seems to generate when silence prevails.

We're in a valley among mountains but can't see them from our porch. Only the cooler air during hot summer months lets us know that we're in the higher regions of the South. What I see from our porch are purple dahlias, the plants rising six to eight feet, trying to keep up with the corn as they both seek the sun. Only two or three day lilies are blooming now, and the purple stalks of the blazing star are fading.

But the loveliest fact of August is that summer isn't really over. Even though many flowers and vegetables have bloomed and produced, their greenery remains as background for late summer blooms. The pink, purple and white rose of sharon are weaving in and out of elderly lilac and forsythia bushes in a wild looking hedge between us and our neighbors. Black-eyed susans next to the garden and pink and white geraniums in two whisky barrel halves at the end of the front pea-gravel walk are thinning out, but still trying.

August is still trying to be summer. Some would say it tries too much with often the hottest, muggiest days of the season. Maybe only someone sitting on a screened porch, wrapped in a housecoat, legs covered by a cotton throw and a warm cat, could be so philosophical about the supposed joys of August. I realize that my ancestor who sat on a front porch in the Georgia midlands, wiping sweat from her forehead and waving a cardboard funeral-home fan, might not have been so fond of this month. But she knew its bounties, too — ripe tomatoes on the vine and watermelons cooling in a nearby creek. And I imagine her, especially in August, finding some peace and quiet on a porch in early morning, looking north to my mountains.

August 7, 1994

A screened porch on a summer Sunday morning is an observation deck. In the hours before humans start engines, heading for lawns, the lake, or the Lord's houses, dogs and cats are prowling, pleasing themselves and upsetting others. The barks and yowls of the home-guarders fill the otherwise peaceful moments. Without the unnatural sights and sounds, peaceful describes this world — a cardinal's springing from limb to limb among the lilac bushes, the crickets' concert from dark underneath places, the bees darting from one rose of sharon blossom to another. The bird chatter or the insect hum seem natural and therefore acceptable, a pleasant background music for musing. But a dog's incessant bark or a car's racing engine is unacceptable, a rude interruption of observations, visual and mental.

Just like the hole in the huge spider web hanging between our power and telephone lines, a gaping hole in the human psyche occurs when there's no time (or place) for observation. The spider can repair the web, reweave and resume her natural acts. Or she can move to other spans of lines and weave anew. Either way, she creates and lives. But leaving a gaping hole means no sustenance, no fulfillment of natural needs, no life.

August 9, 1994

A cool breeze just passed through the porch and moved on. There's stillness again except for a remnant that's ruffling the maple leaves a few feet from the screen. The train's whistle blows and its rumbling along the tracks lasts for a couple of minutes. In the stillness of morning we can hear it clearly, even though the line is a half mile away.

Every morning there is one sound after another, or one sound being added to a constant concert. The cricket serenade is joined by various bird chirps, whistles, or jungle cries. I have never figured out which bird sounds like an extra from a Tarzan film and why it's living in East Tennessee. At some point in an ever-growing curiosity about my co-inhabitors I'll remember to ask someone about that bird.

The older I get the closer I feel to nature. I appreciate it more and want to get to know its creatures better. Some people experience this closeness at an early age, and a small number never seem to. The latter have lost the most. No time given to observing the beauty and wonder of nature leaves too much time for noticing the negative. The "news" is mostly bad news. The human, one of God's creations, has too much invented and destroyed, and too little observed and saved. Viewed from a porch, progress looks and sounds less desirable.

August 20, 1994

Back from a Blue Ridge vacation, I again sit on my own screened porch on a Sunday morning; I've turned on the ceiling fan to simulate the Smokies' air. A soaking summer rain provides coolness, but the humidity of valley air adds another ten degrees. The yard is full of robins, one or two at a time leaving worm-hunting to drink or splash in the bird bath. A couple of those waiting for the bath make do with clean-ups in what must be a small lawn pool invisible to me from the porch.

As I pause to consider that what must be another common occurrence for robins had escaped my attention for fifty years, a thud against the screen made me jump. A female cardinal had hit the screen, bounced to the brick corner post, and landed on the pine chips by the porch. She sat dazed for a few seconds and I involuntarily uttered aloud a sympathetic, "Oh, dear." She shook her head and flew off, out of the yard, in what looked (or I hoped) was a straight, normal path. Almost immediately a male landed in the maple tree a few feet from the porch and sat calling, and calling. He hopped from branch to branch, looking toward different flight paths. Soon he too flew off. Again my hope was that he spotted her, or she him and they met just out of my view. Once more I hear cardinals chirping, and I want to believe in happy endings.

August 26, 1994

That summer is almost over seems very apparent now. The only blooms yet visible from the porch are a few pink dahlias across the driveway, an even smaller number of black-eyed susans, and the blossoms of the angel-wing begonias, in hanging planters. The mother plant sits just outside the screened porch. Its leaves are more rosy than its offspring, perhaps from its better place in the sun.

The plant came from the settlement of my parents' earthly goods. When my father remarried two years after my mother's death and moved into my stepmother's home, plants and other possessions needed new homes. My brother and I spent a weekend sorting and dividing. From that weekend we came away with more treasures than either of us had room for, but were too precious to discard.

On my porch sit a wicker settee and chair, truly antiques since they had belonged to my mother's parents at least as far back as my mother's courting days. Another loveseat, chair and table set complete the seating arrangement. These had already become ours when a neighbor of my parents died, and they passed along to us her bequests. From any of these seats, I can see the night-blooming cactus at the corner of the house, the pink-blossomed justitia, and the begonias. In a corner by the wicker settee sits a weeping fig, a gift from Fred's aunt when my mother died.

It's surprising that I can sit so happily on this porch, surrounded by so many reminders of death — furniture and plants obtained only because of it, and outside plants and trees so obviously on their way to winter. And winter will close the porch. The plants and I will come inside until April, when I'll wash off the wicker, re-pot the plants, and rejoice in past and present summers.

CAROL BROOKS NORRIS is an associate professor and librarian at East Tennessee State University. In addition to poetry, she has written several professional articles, bibliographies, and reviews. Norris lives in Johnson City.

Sue Richardson Orr

It's Just a Tomato

It's just a tomato, right?

Except. . . my grandfather climbed a fence, long before I was born, to steal a big tomato off a plant in a field in Pennsylvania. He brought it back to Tennessee, and instead of eating it, he saved the seeds and planted them the next spring. That was the beginning of the Richardson tomatoes. I didn't find out until the summer of '94 when my parents were sitting around reminiscing one day that there actually was another name, "Mortgage Lifters." That's ironic. Not one plant or tomato has ever been sold by my family, no matter how tight money may have been, but thousands have been freely shared.

It's just a tomato, right?

Except. . . each year my dad has pulled a couple of the biggest and best, two pounds or so, scooped out the seeds, then spread them on an old newspaper to dry. Just like his dad did all those years ago.

It's just a tomato, right?

Except. . . in early March an eighty-plus year old man carefully combines just the right mixture of God's prime dirt and peat moss in a tub that was used for scrubbing his clothes when he was building dams and steam plants for TVA. He plucks each seed gently from the tattered paper and presses it — tenderly — into the waiting soil, telling it to grow. Just like his dad did.

175

It's just a tomato, right?

Except. . . sick children have received less care than the spindly, wee plants that emerge from the saved seeds in only a few days time. They wriggle up through the moist dark to sunlight, then lean their faces to the warmth so intently the tub has to be rotated 180 degrees twice a day to keep them growing straight and true.

It's just a tomato, right?

Except. . . our family friend, Dorothy, who had worked at the school cafeteria since before I went through the line, brought sacks of half-pint milk cartons to Dad every winter until she died. After that, he had to go knock on the cafeteria manager's door and explain his need for hundreds of empty cartons because that's where his tomatoes slept! He probably even promised her a few plants. She started bringing them to him, so he could fill them with his special mixture, then lift the three-inch plants out of the nursery tub into homes of their own.

It's just a tomato, right?

Except. . . Dad builds an elaborate three-foot high greenhouse with layers of plastic topped with a tarp and heated by a 100-watt bulb for these seedlings. As the day warms, he peels back covers; then, in the after-sunset chill, he tucks them around again, just so. None of us—children or grandchildren, certainly not great-grands—can be trusted with greenhouse duty without careful, specific instructions on how to prop the corner up and when to turn off the bulb. There is only one way.

It's just a tomato, right?

Except. . . the line begins to form in early May, of folks who once again need just a few plants, or six, or twelve. Of course, each year there are new faces in the line. Faces who tasted a Richardson tomato somewhere from Florida to Mississippi to East Tennessee to, for a while, Chicago and Virginia. Dad doles them out, along with advice on how to prepare the site, how to cut the bottom out of the carton, then pull it up around the tender trunk to protect it from cutworms. The one time I bought tomatoes at the Co-op and planted them—without that wax collar—something snipped them all the first night, leaving surprised stubs.

It's just a tomato, right?

Except. . . once the young plants are shared with everyone from granddaughters to a preacher's wife, the race to ripe begins. Every family phone call includes a tomato status report from first bloom to fried green to two-pound ready. They grow tall, six feet if you keep them staked. All over the ground if you don't. They aren't rot resistant or disease resistant, 'cause the seeds have been in the family since before tomatoes were bred to be resistant to anything. You have to spray them fervently, love them with Vigoro, and as Dad says, "Give them chocolate candy and coffee."

It's just a tomato, right?

Except. . . they are wonderful, fresh picked and still warm, when you open wide and sink your teeth in and drip liquid red and bits of gold down the front of your T-shirt. Salads sing when you cube one into them. Once slice covers a whole piece of bread, and the first bite makes you barefoot and eleven. BLT's on sourdough are in a perpetual tie for first with homemade ice cream and watermelon for the best taste of summer. In winter, when you thaw a frozen package and cook them for spaghetti sauce, the kitchen smells like July and you want to call Dad and say, "Mine are ripe!"

It's just a tomato, right?

Except. . . Dad won't leave home for an overnight, hardly for an all day, from the time he puts the seeds to soil until he has them planted in the garden, a foot tall and secured to an eight-foot stake with soft strips from old longjohns. The tomato process is a task of love for him, of continuity with his past.

It matters more than dogwoods in Knoxville, grandkids in Florida, pilgrimages in Mississippi. More than everything except his wife of sixty-two years, "Miss Edna." So he stays home and tends his plants. Perhaps it is part of what keeps him a busy, spry eighty-six year old who vows to live to be one-hundred. He will probably be nurturing Richardson tomatoes the spring he is. His concern is who will take the tomato torch from his big, caring hands.

It's just a tomato, that's right.

From A Memory Lane

I see a tall, lean woman walking down a narrow gravel road carrying a cane without a crook. Her cotton stockings wrinkle down her legs, then fold into the tops of her dusty brogans. She has on a wash dress with a muted pattern, covered by a fresh apron that ties both behind her neck and waist. She wears a long-sleeved sweater, dingy gray, in both winter and summer, and a floppy bonnet with a brim wide enough to shade her face. Frizzled gray hairs break free around the bonnet's edge.

Aunt Daisy puts a bit of weight on the cane as she steps along, but I know she carries it in case a rattler should slip out from under the big log at the branch. Some have before. . .and died.

She comes down the lane from her log cabin because the family has gathered at Mammy's house for a reunion. For fried chicken, mutton, corn bread, sliced tomatoes, Southern green beans and skillet corn. For hugs, catching up, kick the can, perhaps a trip to the Buffalo for a swim with Uncle Pat. For standing in the shade laughing at Uncle Guy and Uncle Earl and putting our hands in a tub of ice to find a Grapette. For a long walk with a favorite cousin down to the well for a bucket of water, deep-earth cold.

Aunt Daisy sits away from the activities, her cane propped like a queen's staff at court. But I know she is there. When she singles me out and wants me to sit on her knee, or at least nearby to listen for a while, I squirm till I can get away. I'm scared of her, so is my sister, so are my cousins.

Her voice is harsh, no matter what she's saying. And her

chin wiggles when she speaks till I stare in awe to see if it will touch her nose. Her teeth are gone. The store-bought ones never fit well enough to wear, so her occasional laughter reveals gums chewed smooth, stained snuff brown.

I spend my time watching how she talks, never hearing what she has to say.

The smell of old wraps around her—not unpleasant, but not a smell I want to plunge my nose into like Mammy's. Mammy's smell is alive—chicken and dumplings, green onions, woodstove cooking sweat. Aunt Daisy smells of yesterday, and, maybe, never was.

Aunt Daisy is Mammy's youngest sister. She devoted her life to her father, my Great Grandpa Witherspoon. Never married, though several fellows came courting up that hollow to the log house with a dogtrot. Now she lives there alone with Brownie, her mean old dog. I'm scared of him, too.

When my mother was a child, she had to take her turn going to stay for a week with Aunt Daisy to help out with chores and care for her Grandpa. To haul water from the cistern, to carry slops to the two pigs out back, to scatter cracked corn to the chattering Rhode Island Reds, to wring the muslin sheets out by hand and hang them on the line running between the oak and the elm.

Grandpa would sit by the fire in a low, cane-backed chair telling tales from his days as a Rebel soldier. He would poke my mother and say, "You ain't listening, Edny, you ain't listening." She cried herself to sleep every night that she was away from the warm and rowdy fellowship of her nine brothers and sisters.

I cannot imagine spending the night there. It is dark, dusty and somewhere between mysterious and scary. There is a big room on either side of the dogtrot, and since Grandpa died, Aunt Daisy lives only in the one on the right. Years of woodsmoke greet me when I go through the door, and when I think of being there I remember more impressions than details

There is an unsteady kitchen table shoved against the

wall. On it there is an enamel bucket full of water with a metal dipper hanging on the rim, a coal oil lamp, perhaps a plate of corn bread. Aunt Daisy's bed is in one corner, the rough-hewn headboard aged soft. Grandpa made it when he and my Great Grandmother set up housekeeping. A couple of wood chairs, one tall rocker, and a three-legged stool are settled around the room.

The yard is worn to dirt around the house and the log walls sag into U's at mid-beam. No telling how long they have been there. That was probably one of the stories I squirmed through.

I have never walked all the way from Mammy's to Aunt Daisy's alone. I've tried a few times, but I always come back after I cross the branch and get to the long stretch where I can't see either cabin. Fear of "something getting me," knowing too many snake tales, who knows? I do know it's the longest half mile in the world.

Perhaps because it goes from here to somewhere I don't want to be.

SUE RICHARDSON ORR grew up in the hills of middle Tennessee near Kentucky Lake, but now lives in Madisonville on a hill overlooking her vineyard.

Linda Parsons

Aura

My aura is different from a hundred
others, the psychic tells me. Not smooth
and cradling my body like a spoon, but
shooting out in arrows of yellow and gold.
Not that I pop light bulbs or find missing
persons, but young children and animals
are drawn to my shiny edges. Not that
my heart is soft and wears well on my sleeve,
but the troubled, the tired, the poor seek me
out in the blindest alley. Not that I give
too freely and take too little, but I'm learning
how to balance this ball and five cups
on my nose. Not that my rooms are very neat,
but I took small things from my grandmother's
house, things no one else claimed, that would fit
in your hand — me at six, me at eight, me at ten.
Not that I cry at drums in parades, but
the memory of Treblinka weighs me down
like a brick. Not that I lived in one place
longer than a year growing up, once above
an Esso station where axle grease and catcalls
were my perfume. But now I recognize
other orphans when we meet on the street.
And not that I want all this gold for myself,
this signal, this brief news of good.
Not that I want it at all.

LINDA PARSONS is poetry editor of *Now & Then* magazine, and is the
recipient of the 1995 Tennessee Poetry Prize. Her poems have
appeared in numerous publications over the years, and her first collection is forthcoming from Sow's Ear Press. Parsons is an editor and
policy analyst at the University of Tennessee at Knoxville.

Thomas S. Rich

Snowflakes

I remember carrying a basket of food for the
Hickersons, a day like this, with my father
up a winding steep road to a cabin hidden

among the snow-filled hills and clambering
Tennessee pines, near Livingston,
when gentle snowflakes dropped as if

from an overturned basket in the sky —
large white crystals falling, drifting slowly
downward to cover tired brown grass,

to settle softly on winter withered limbs,
covering our tracks, cabin roof, layering the
slumbering woods to silence, except for

crunching boots. I remember the childrens'
dirty faces peering at us when we gave them
our basket, dull eyes — lumps of coal — puzzled

stares and their mother laughing, then crying.
At twelve, I did not understand alcoholism,
abuse, neglect, but did feel the utter coldness

of the cabin, smell the dirt floor, saw a
ragged doll without a head, a room without
a Christmas tree. . .

Snowflakes falling, covering the land
as night now covers this day. Earth
letting go. Silent steps covered in white.

THOMAS S. RICH lives in Nashville and admits that he is new to writing poetry, beginning two years ago as a way to express the emotional cost of dealing with his mother's Alzheimer's disease.

Jeff Shearer

Loose Lips

No offense, honey, but I'm sure glad you're my last appointment. This has been one *hellacious* day, pardon my French. Right over here. Can you lean back just a little further? This shampoo's herbal, but it's *nasty* if it gets in your eyes.

So what brings you to our humble little hamlet?

Getting married? Oh, someone's a *very* lucky man. You must be excited. For a moment I thought you were part of one of those news crews. Honey, Jimmy Hoffa could have been shacked up with Elvis the way reporters have been tracing through here. You haven't heard? It's like the whole community is *unraveling*. Everyone who's someone has been in some sort of scandal lately. The Kellers are the ones that have the media hopping this week. It's like some horrid "We can do Better than Bobbitt" contest, only Mrs. Keller seems to have had a better pitching arm. To think that for years this town tried to find some way to get listed in the Triple-A guide. What's that Chinese proverb—don't wish for something too hard, because you might just get it? Well darling, cross my heart and hope to die, the Chinese were right. You may quote me wildly on that.

Of course, all I know is what I hear. And in this line of work, loose lips lose tips. You just can't afford to be a chatterbox and expect to have a loyal clientele. But to be perfectly honest, my business has never been better since the phone company did away with all the party lines. Bless you, Ma Bell, bless you. Ker-ching, ker-ching. I'd be a pauper if people had some other way to get the latest gossip. Here comes the chamomile rinse. Don't you just love that smell? Umm, I think it's divine.

My name? Harold. Actually it's Harry, but mums the word, promise? Swear to God, my birth certificate says "Harry." "Harry" sounds so much like a primate, don't you think? I've been Harold since I was twelve. Second rinse, dear. You've got magnificent roots, has anyone ever told you that?

This town? Quaint? As my favorite author would say — honey, don't let me *commence*. You mention Truman around here and they think you're talking about that perky little president. Capote is something you put on toast. I kid you not. If you took a survey, I bet Oscar Wilde would show up as a tight end for the Cowboys. *S'il vous plait*, don't get me started.

Me? Highly recommended? Oh please, don't tease. Actually, I think I knew what I wanted to do since I was ten. While other boys were off sneaking copies of Playboy from their father's top drawer, I was reading Vanity Fair. Honey, I'm here to tell you this place was suffering from fashion *deprivation*. I swear to God, lava lamps on chrome coffee tables were haute couture.

Furniture, though, was nothing compared to the frumpy hairstyles and constipated clothes you could find here. I used to sit in the back row of church with my friend Robert. The last pew is the ideal spot for hair review. It's like inspecting the troops, you know, only from behind. We had a code for anything we'd like to banish: "Snip, snip." Oh, we had fun — church was practically a party with Robert around. Anyway, as people filed in, we'd throw fashion flags right and left. "Snip, snip! Too heavy on the mousse. Penalty! Purple glitter in a starburst perm! Mayonnaise shampoo? Personal foul? Smells like tuna salad on a hot tin roof! Snip, snip!" Honey, I'm here to tell you, it was *sacrilegious* what they did to their hair. Robert had to cover my mouth once to keep me from yelling "Jesus Christ!" right in the middle of the offering. *God*, I miss him.

My parents? Girl, I loved them to death, but they never knew what hit them in the delivery room. I guess they did the best they could with what fell into their laps. Poor Father. He had dreams of glory for his little Harry. His dream simply never included a son who couldn't catch a pass with a Velcro ball. Yes, you could say he was just a *wee* disappointed. Ooh, the memories. I heard him shouting at my mother one night. This was after one of my weekly run-ins with the local mole patrol. I'll never forget the frustration in his voice: "He just stood there and took it, Shirley. I yelled at him to swing back. `Don't just stand there, Harry. Hit him! Hit him back." Good God, Shirley, he just stood there and took it. I don't understand it. I *just don't* get it." Oh, Father was furious.

But that's all distant diary. Besides, you can't bite the hand that feeds you, right? I'm just glad I've got something I feel drawn to. Look at the alternative. Could you see me in a Sears suit and wingtips? Please us, Jesus! I'd sell Mary Kay before I'd do that.

Listen to me, flapping my gums. Earth to Harold, Earth to Harold. Sit up a little, honey. I want to see if we can give your ends a flirty little flip. There. We'll add some molding creme later to keep that sexy fringe from getting out of hand.

The scandal? I can't think of a soul who hasn't been touched by it. It's a veritable epidemic, that's what it is. The nasty business with the Kellers is the only thing people have talked about all week. And that's just the latest episode. What's that saying—it's deja vu all over again? Mrs. Keller used to be one of my regulars, you know. Every second Monday, four o'clock. Mr. Keller was supposed to be golfing, but I heard— and mind you this is only what I heard—that the one Monday I had to close early is the day the Missus finds Mr. Keller practicing with his little putter *off the course*, if you know what I mean. Lean a little to the right. That's good. I guess they'll miss him at the clubhouse. And such a civic leader, to boot.

Like I said, honey, it's an epidemic. A real sticky wicket, as the Brits would say. Did you hear about that little business with the Batsons? No? Oh, Lordy, Miss Lordy, what a story for the Globe. The Batsons were supposed to be the town's little Shake-and-Bake couple. I went to school with Jerry Batson. They were the June and Ward type, you know? Had a son—

186

guess that would make him the Beaver, wouldn't it? Oh, honey, don't let me *commence*. Anyway, Mrs. Batson was going to surprise Mr. B with a little birthday party at the office. Everyone was supposed to keep it a secret. Oh, girl, she was all fuss and feathers over the idea—even had the Mayor promise to show up. The only thing is, Mr. B's secretary was out that day. Well, when the whole birthday crew comes busting through the door to his office with cake and streamers, Mr. B is sitting there in the buff with a young nymphet from Human Resources between his legs proving just how resourceful she could be. God, wouldn't you just *die* to have seen his face? That's one birthday party he'll never forget—lost everything he owned just from wanting someone to blow out his candle.

Poor timing? Oh, honey, that is an *understatement*. But the timing thing is what is so utterly spooky about his whole nasty business. It's like this town has—oh, what is the word? You know, the ability to find something by lucky accident? Yes—*serendipity*, that's it. Thank you, Ms. Webster. *Serendipity*. Only I suppose the jury's still out on the word lucky, right?

When did this all begin? Let's see. The first little episode would have to be the Andersons. No—that's not right. It was the Beans. The reason I remember is that I had Coach Bean in school. A veritable *barbarian*. Robert and I called him Budweiser Brain. Snip, snip! I'll never forget the day I refused to dress down for PE. Coach Bean, he orders me to strip. He's holding this size 12 tennis shoe, tapping it against his chubby little fist like so. Tennis shoes don't leave marks, you know. So I'm standing there, and he keeps telling me, "Pull 'em down, son, or I'll have 'em pulled down for ya." I don't say anything. Just stand there with my arms folded. It was dodgeball day, you see, and I had just decided I was not going to let myself be their practice target any more.

Coach Bean was *furious*."That's the way you want it?" I still wouldn't say a word. I just looked at him. He went over and turned on the cold water. When he came back, he got right up in my face. He was so red I could feel the heat. Then he said,

"OK, boys, help him off with 'em." Excuse me. I need to catch my breath. Oo-wee. I'm sorry, but do you have any idea what it feels like to be undressed by twenty pairs of hands? Grabbing, *mauling* hands. God, honey, I get the hives just thinking about it. But I did not cry. Oh, the urge was overwhelming, but I fought it. The coach dumped the balls out of a bag right there in the locker room. The only thing I remember after that is being hunched up in the corner of the shower, naked as a baby. The cold water numbed me to the point that I never felt the balls hit me. I just remember the sound they made. Over and over and over. But I did *not* cry. Not a tear. Oh, were they disappointed. Tilt back now. There, that's fine. These rollers are great for giving you a sort of spunky panache.

My parents? Oh, honey, you shouldn't have asked. That night my father heard what happened and went to confront Coach Bean. I don't know how he found out. I never said anything. That's when Coach Bean told him some *horrid* little story they'd made up about Robert and me. When he came home, I was supposed to be in bed. Oh, how my parents yelled that night. And you know, my father never even asked me. That's what I don't understand. He *never* asked me if it were true. I think he was scared. Isn't that pitiful? Afraid to ask your own son.

Well, that was on a Friday. And the very next evening there's a meeting of the school board to decide how to handle the Harry and Robert situation. My parents went. My mother tried to convince Robert's mother to go, but she was too frightened. When we got there, the school board already had a solution to the whole thing. They were going to put the two of us into a special class. "Varied Exceptionalities." Isn't that a hoot? You've got to give them credit for the polysyllabic solution. My father was so furious he kept yelling at them, even after the meeting had adjourned and everyone was gone except for Mother and me. "He not like that! My son is not like that!" God, I can still hear him. And we were the only ones there.

I was the one who found Robert the next morning. I

knew something was wrong when he didn't show up for church. He did it in the attic. No letter to his mother, nothing. And I remember thinking when I found him — how curious, he's frowning. I expected something more like rage. That's the memory I have — being disappointed that it was just a frown.

Oh, honey, listen to me flapping my gums about such a morbid little walk down memory lane. Why did we stay? My father didn't. He left the house to Mother, but she could never find a buyer. At least that was her excuse. Between you and me, I think she refused to leave. She didn't want to give them the pleasure of our absence from their happy little hamlet. Hold the mirror, sugar, I want to show you how the off-center part is going to frame your face. See how this hugs your fabulous cheekbones? Never underestimate the power of a hairdresser.

Enough about me. You have *got* to be simply moist with excitement, getting married and all. Second thoughts? Girl, don't you dare. Like my father used to say, if you've got half a heart, you'll finish what you start. Isn't that ironic. It's the only thing he taught me that stuck, and he's not around to hear me quote him. So, you never told me, who's the lucky man? Randy Simms? Girl, get out of here! What a small world. I went to school with Randy. Oh, I'm sure he remembers me. But that was long before I became the messiah of mousse. Secrets? Now, honey, remember what I said, loose lips lose tips. You'll find out whatever secrets you need to know soon enough. Oh, I'm so *excited* for you!

Gift for the groom? Oh, sugar, I wouldn't know where to start. But I know someone who can help you. Sandy Powell, she's a regular of mine. She and Randy were close in high school. Randy and Sandy. They were two peas in a pod. If anyone could tell you what would make Randy smile, she's the one. She's in the first condo by the park. You can't miss it. And I have it on impeccable authority that she gets off work just about now. You see her, and you won't go wrong with a gift for Randy.

Ooh, look at the time. You'd better hustle buns, beet

cheeks, if you're going to meet Sandy. If she doesn't answer, just poke your head in the door and give her a little yoo-hoo. That's the advantage of living in such a small town — we may have a few boors, but we don't lock our doors.

What's that? Still nervous? Girl, you're going to do just fine. Don't let me see that pretty face looking like Polly Paranoia. You just keep that one thought front and center — if you have half a heart, you'll finish what you start.

There you go. You like? Remember, now, blow dry and lightly spritz. No, no — put that money away, this is my treat. In this line of work, compensation is sometimes just getting to watch the results, and I've never felt underpaid. Tell you what, when you see that lucky man of yours, be sure to tell him Harold said "hi."

One more look before you go. What's that, a "knock-out"? Girl, call me smug and give me a hug, but *knock-out* simply doesn't do justice to what we just created. This may be Dog Patch, honey, but what we have here is nothing less than one *killer* do.

Double Yellow Lines

Someone once called Palmer a classic example of a dying mining town. When Sheriff Collins heard that he said, "Dying, hell. This town has had rigor mortis for forty years."

And maybe that's what keeps us here, hanging on. Because when you no longer have to worry about making it or not making it, you put a lot tighter grip on what little you're left holding. Like early last fall, when they finally painted double yellow lines up State 56 to the junction. You would've thought that was going to be Palmer's event of the year the way we carried on about it. But that seems like nothing now, compared to what happened later to Walter Armfield.

We could never figure out why anyone would make such a fuss over a man's age when it came to his ability to drive. Sheriff Collins was set in his tracks, though. He said he wasn't going to have it on his conscience if Walter Armfield killed himself or somebody else on his drive down the mountain for his weekly visit to the Palmer Black Lung Clinic and then back over to the Ready-Set-Go for his carton of Camel Straights. He said it was high time Walter got himself a driver's license.

We had all heard the conversation between Walter and Sheriff Collins so many times that we had it memorized.

First Collins would ask Walter, "You going to pass that test on the first try, Walter?"

Then Walter would say, "Good God. If a man hasn't learned to drive after 70 years, there's no damn test that's going to teach him now."

And then Collins was supposed to say, "It's never too

late to start doing things right."

That's when Walter would counter with "I'll tell you about doing things right. You take these kids today with their cars. You have them start out driving a team the way I did. You can't even find me a teamster now days who's ever been behind a team. A car ain't nothing compared to a team of kicking, pulling mules. Teamsters my ass."

Then Collins always finished with "Walter, I'm more worried about you passing that eye test than I am about you reciting the five shapes of roadsigns. Better get those glasses checked out before you go apply for that license."

That's the point where Walter would roll his eyes and kind of wink real hard— only it wasn't a wink, it was some sort of tic he had whenever he got excited. And then he'd turn and walk away.

When Walter turned 90 last month, we wanted to throw him a party, but he wouldn't have it. He said he was too busy studying what he called his little book— that driver's manual the state sent him. He was worrying himself sick about passing that test. His great granddaughter Maggie had been up to his house every day after school, going over the questions with him. They would do that for an hour and then he would have her lay out a line of pine cones, after which he would set about trying to parallel park between them. Maggie said he had gotten it down to just two smashed cones.

We watched this go on for about two weeks when we all decided to take the matter up with Sheriff Collins. Because everyone who knew Walter knew that the only two things that kept him from nailing his own coffin shut were that '53 Plymouth and that great granddaughter of his.

That's when we told Sheriff Collins that if he wanted to protect the county from reckless endangerment then Walter Armfield wasn't the one he should be worried about. He should be figuring out a way to deal with Buddy. Buddy Ainsworth. That boy has been tormenting this town ever since his mother left him behind here, after finding herself a man who was willing to take her away from the place that she called God's idea of a bad joke. We said good riddance when she left, but not good enough, because now we had Buddy to deal with.

Buddy was sixteen when his mother took off, leaving him the trailer, a three-quarter ton pickup, and a half empty bottle of *Old Crow*. We knew he was mean before she ran off, but afterwards, he wore his meanness like some kind of badge.

Everybody in this town has a Buddy Ainsworth story to tell. Mostly it's damage to person or property— if he hasn't run them off the road, then he's run over their dog. But sometimes it's just out-and-out spit-in-your-eye meanness.

The Jameson twins still talk about the time they were out playing in their yard when Buddy drove up and asked them if they wanted some free kittens. Said he found them under his trailer and couldn't find the mamma cat. When they came up close he tossed them a burlap bag, said "You give 'em a good home, now," and drove off. The twins said all six kittens they found in that bag were dead. Besides that, they both swore they could see his face in that big old side mirror of his as he drove off. He was laughing.

Buddy and that truck were forever getting into trouble with the law. And the thing that got us was how he always managed to worm his way out from any serious consequence. The guy who drives that tractor rig in here once a month to pick up scrap metal said he had heard about Buddy two counties over. He said he had it on good authority that Buddy had been pulled over by two deputies, and that when they tried to cuff him, he ended up turning out the lights on both of those fellas. They never even tried to prosecute. Sheriff Collins said it was a matter of pride.

Even the people over in Coalton hated Buddy. The daughter of the Baptist preacher over there made the mistake of going alone to confront Buddy when she found out the reason why her clothes suddenly no longer fit. Later that day, when they tended to her at the clinic, all she would tell them was that she fell getting out of his truck. The nurse who looked her over said it was the worst case of head trauma she'd ever seen attributed to a non-moving vehicle. That same accident, they wrote in her records, also terminated the condition that caused her to confront Buddy in the first place. Without the girl pressing charges, of course, they couldn't touch Buddy. Everyone noticed, though, when the message that had been on the port-a-sign in front of the Baptist church was suddenly taken off. The message had been up all month and read: "Those least deserving forgiveness are those that need it most." Nobody asked the preacher why he hadn't replaced the message.

Then last May, we thought we had a day going that not even Buddy could mess up. The air was crisp, and the locust trees were in full bloom, giving the whole town a bath in the sweetest smelling fragrance you'll find in the whole county, maybe the whole state. Those of us at the Ready-Set-Go were laughing and carrying on like it was some kind of holiday. Wylie— he owns the place— he had us in tears we were laughing so hard.

Of course we tempered it down when little Maggie Armfield came in. "You still helping your granddaddy with his driving lessons?" Wylie asked her.

She shoved a handful of candy and a couple of quarters on the counter. "Yessir. Today we're doing yielding and merging."

We all chuckled. Wylie said, "Your granddaddy must be fixin' to do some real traveling if he's going to get anywhere close to where he needs to know about yielding and merging."

Pushing open the screen door, that little Maggie didn't even look back. She just said, "Great granddaddy doesn't want to be no horse's ass."

You should have seen the expression on Wylie's face. He didn't have a come-back for that, and that just set us off again. We were laughing so hard that at first we didn't hear the horn. But we did hear the brakes. The lot of us took one look at each other and were out that door before his truck even came to a stop. We had to climb over the guard rail and a fence before we finally found her. She was lying under a bunch of honeysuckle. Roger Hightower was the first to see her, and the way he said "Oh, Jesus", we knew there was no need to call for an ambulance.

We just stood there— none of us knew what to say. That's when we saw Buddy backing up his truck. Swear to God he never even got out of it. Backed it up parallel to where we were all standing, leaned out the window and shouted, "Tell Collins that if he's looking for me I'll be up at my place."

He started to drive off but stopped, leaned out again and yelled, "She shouldn't a been crossin' there, you know. Should have crossed down by the grange. You don't cross against double yellow lines." Then he took off. Just like that. Like he'd done nothing more than hit some stray dog.

When Buddy's trial came up they had to bring in extra chairs from the grange hall to accommodate all of us that showed up. The judge they sent over to hear the case was a new one to the circuit. That worried Mr. Morgan— he's the prosecutor— but there was no way we thought Buddy could ever worm his way out of this one.

The trial lasted two days. We thought Buddy's lawyer was never going to shut up. He kept harping about Buddy being a minor, and how the whole proceeding was against some state statute because Buddy didn't have his legal guardian present. We couldn't believe the judge could listen to this with a straight face. Someone said even if Buddy's mother had shown up, she probably would have sided with the prosecution. A lot of the talking was over our heads, but no one who had managed to find a chair was willing to give it up even during breaks, afraid that he'd miss getting to hear the judge throw the book at Buddy.

At the end of the second day, Buddy's attorney must have run out of things to say, and that's when the judge asked them both to wrap it all up, which they promptly did.

After a ten minute recess, the judge called both attorneys up to the bench, waved his finger at each of them like they were misbehaved kids, and promptly sent them back to their chairs. He then said he was granting an adjournment comtemplating a dismissal. And then he had the bailiff escort Buddy out the door.

Of course we were all waiting to hear Mr. Morgan explain how all that was going to translate into a real sentence, but Mr. Morgan just sat there shaking his head and tapping his pencil hard on his big yellow pad.

We asked him what the matter was, and asked him when the judge was going to get around to declaring a length of sentence. But that's when he told us there would be no sentence. That the judge was calling it shared negligence. He was calling the county negligent for ever letting Buddy live by himself in the first place. And that's why he was letting Buddy go as long as he promised to behave himself for a year. Mr. Morgan looked like he was about to cry in shame, and we were all real quiet, not knowing what to do, when from outside came a laugh that none of us failed to recognize — a screechy laugh like a mating raccoon. It was Buddy. It was like he had to rub it in our faces — like he was beyond even faking remorse.

Well, after that, we didn't see Walter for close to a month. Social Services sent some people up to look in on him. He wouldn't let them in, though. Told them not to waste their time on a worthless old horse's ass like him.

He did show himself, though, when a bunch of us called a meeting to look at taking take care of Buddy once and for all. The only trouble was, word had also gotten out to Sheriff Collins, and we weren't ten minutes into the meeting when Collins walks in and stands in the back with his arms folded. He listened to two, maybe three of us, before he decided he had heard enough, and then interrupted Roger Hightower who had been talking nonstop about what he could do if just given five minutes alone with that boy.

"I understand how all of you feel." Collins said. "I feel just as mad as you do. And you know I've been after Buddy long before this happened."

He stopped and surveyed the room full of faces. "But I want to see the hands of each of you who is ready to go home to your family and explain that they won't be seeing any more of you because you felt you had to do something the law was too slow to do."

He looked at each of us again. "Well, anybody ready to do that?" None of us would look him in the face. "Course not. And you'd be damn fools if you were. You leave this to the county prosecutor and me. We're looking at another charge against him right now. You just let us take care of Buddy." This must have been too much for Walter to handle, because that's when we saw him get up from his chair and head for the door. It wasn't much of a meeting after that, and we all went home feeling worse than before we came.

It was the following Friday when we got the news. We were standing around the Ready-Set-Go, none of us feeling much like cuttin' up the way we used to, when Wylie's boy comes in. Said he saw the whole thing.

Apparently he was heading up 56 when Buddy came out of nowhere and passed him like he was standing still. And not a mile after that, at the foot of the hill, he sees a car pull out right in front of Buddy's truck. He said Buddy almost rear-ended the guy.

He could tell Buddy was angry as hell at being stuck like that. Said Buddy got right up behind that car in front and really laid on the horn. The two of them weren't going more than 30 up that road — too many S-curves to do more than that. And every time Buddy would swing out to pass, they'd be right on top of another curve and he'd back off. There's just no way to see if anything's coming on that stretch.

Buddy must have been in some kind of hurry according to Wylie's boy, because this went on all the way up to the top of the grade — Buddy making a move to pass, but pulling back in at the last second. So when that car in front pulled around the last turn and reached the top of the hill, Wylie's boy said he could see an arm reach out of the driver's window real slow like and give the all-clear-ahead sign to Buddy. And Buddy didn't waste any time. He saw that hand waving him on and stepped on it.

The driver of the tractor rig said he never even had a chance to hit the brakes when he saw Buddy's truck. Said he was doing close to 50 and that Buddy had to be doing at least the same. When they finally managed to get Buddy out of what was left of his truck, for the second time in twice as many months there was no need to put a call in for an ambulance.

Wiley's boy said Walter sat on the front bumper of his car, lit up one of those Camel Straights, and watched them work on cleaning up the wreck. Didn't say a thing the whole time.

When Sheriff Collins finally got there he heard the whole story from Wylie's boy, then talked to the driver of the tractor rig. After that he walked over to Walter and put his hand on his shoulder. Walter just looked up at him. Neither one said anything for the longest time. Then Walter got up, put his hat on, and said, "Guess you were right, Collins. Guess it's time to get these glasses checked."

Whenever Sheriff Collins tells the story— and he's asked to tell it often— he never lets on. He never lets on as to whether he thinks that look that Walter gave him on climbing back into that Plymouth— whether it was that tic of his, or a wink.

JEFF SHEARER was the 1995 first place winner in TWA' s fiction contest. A recent story, *Grand Opening*, will appear in the magazine *Now & Then*. Shearer makes his home in Nashville.

Patricia Shirley

Tennessee Tatting

In current fashion, I decorate my armoire
with Great-Grandma Rachel's cambric blouse,
and admire the clever lace she knotted
in the rage of antiqued days.
Before my single memory of this ancient,
slowed by arthritis and lost sight,
her silver shuttle looped mazy perfection,
unmindful that Chinese or Egyptians created
the skill of rings, and squares, and stars
that Madame de Pompadour fancied into frivolite.
The style bridges time with elegance.
Fascinated, I'm urged to taut fine thread,
hopscotching to a graceful time when
supple fingers flashed the shuttle through
rows of grapevine and edgings of Ball and Chain.

PATRICIA SHIRLEY is the creator of a character named Pearl, who
appears in *Pearl* and *Mary Pearl Kline*. She is the 1996 president of the
Knoxville Writer's Group, and reads her poetry and stories on radio
station WUOT in Knoxville.

Milton Stanley

Secret City

Sherb McKinney moved along the hillside to the next sapling in a row of peach trees, drove a shovel blade into the ground and pushed it down to the handle with his boot. He did the same on the other sides of the tree, on the last one pulling up an inverted pyramid of roots and rocky soil and depositing it, along with the chest-high trunk, onto a patch of burlap his son Levi dropped from a sack onto the ground.

The boy pulled a short pre-cut strip of twine from the pocket of his trousers and tied it around the tiny trunk to secure the roots in a neat, elongated ball, then dropped it into a rusty brown wheelbarrow he rolled behind his father. When the little peach saplings, covered with thousands of leaf buds, filled the wheelbarrow, Levi took them back toward the barn.

The boy held tightly to the loaded wheelbarrow that threatened to take off without him down the steep hill. He was as big as his father now, short and lean with forearms suntanned and muscled like honeysuckle vines. Except for the mustache and pepper-gray around his father's temples, the two could pass as twins, separated by thirty years. Since starting at the high school in Clinton, Levi had only been able to help his father a couple of hours each a day. Next year Lillie would be going to the high school too. Sending them both would be a sacrifice, but in a couple of years Verna would be old enough to work in the garden. By the time she was grown the two little ones would be old enough to help.

The garden, barn and house—a two-room white frame building with an attic bedroom—were located down at the front of the property. The peach trees were farther up the hill in two sections: Carman on the east end, Elberta on the north. Sherb was proud of the living he had made growing them. He knew it would be pointless going head-to-head against Dyllis Orchard and the other big outfits selling fruit, so he challenged them at the source—with a nursery. By his estimate he had sold close to 5,000 trees in eight years—more than a few to the big outfits themselves.

In that time he had come to love his new home as much as the one his people had been forced to leave in Union County—25 acres of bottomland so secluded and wild there wasn't even a name for that part of the county. In 1935 TVA and the Norris Dam project—Sherb called it Damn Norris—came and scattered his family: his uncle and cousins to Kentucky; Sherb, Martha and the children down the Clinch River to 30 acres on Blackoak Ridge near Oliver Springs. The hilltop property had been all he could afford on his condemnation check, but he cherished a spot far enough up from the river he would never have to worry about another eviction from TVA.

He hadn't made allowance for the Army, which was again asking him to sacrifice for a world war, this time by turning his property over for something so secret no one would say why the government needed it at all. He now had less than three weeks to move out, and no idea where his family would go.

He would miss the view this time of afternoon, when the sun was low enough to pour a copper shine over the oaks and pines in the entire East Fork Valley.

Dozers and dump trucks ground and smoked to the east, sending up lines of dust and diesel exhaust that hung in a thin cloud over the entire floodplain between Blackoak and East Fork ridges. Every day the machinery tore its way through more countryside, driving out families which had been there a hundred years and throwing up street after street of identical frame houses like sprouts in a plow row. Highway 61 to Kingston was closed—soldiers and German shepherds at checkpoints turning cars away without a word of explanation.

Sherb squatted under pretense of tying a bootlace and rested his back. Where he sat he was invisible among the rows of new growth. A gust of wind made its way up from the southwest, starting low and far-off, rising in a gentle crescendo until it filled the whole valley and swept away all other sounds. Sherb closed his eyes and drank in the wind that, while it lasted, carried him into a timelessness that at some unspoken level he associated with heaven.

After a few minutes, the wind blew on up the valley and the sound of its moving through the trees faded, giving way to the familiar clack and rattle of the wheelbarrow making its way back up the hill. Sherb finished tying his leather bootlace in a double bow and used the shovel to push himself to his feet.

Walking beside Levi was a tall man in a woolen Army uniform—green with a khaki tie tucked in neatly at the chest. He was a young man with broad shoulders and the insignia of an engineer lieutenant on his collar. In one hand he carried a long roll of papers. For a moment Sherb was afraid Levi had enlisted. The boy was 17 and wanted badly to join the Army, but his father wanted even more to keep him in school. Sherb had volunteered for the 117th National Guard regiment during the Pancho Villa expedition. He spent a year in camp in Pennsylvania, where the men got poorer and sicker while the officers drew fat paychecks and lied to their superiors about morale. The next year Sherb was sent with the 117th to France as a supply clerk. He never saw combat, but lost enough friends to appreciate war's rock-bottom reality. He had no intention of losing his son and was afraid pulling Levi out of school would be all it took for him to enlist.

"Good afternoon, Mr. McKinney. I'm Lieutenant Delacroix from the Land Acquisition Section," the young man said without looking directly at Sherb. He spoke with a Northern accent Sherb vaguely associated with New York—rude and intolerant of Southerners. He had a pencil-line mustache traced along the top of his upper lip and smelled of

Listerine and rose pomade.

"Good afternoon, Lieutenant," Sherb said far more cordially than he felt. He wiped his hand quickly across the leg of his overalls and extended it; the man looked down at it for a moment before giving it a perfunctory pump.

"Mr. McKinney, we're very sorry, but we've had a change in our requirements. We need a portion of your property a little sooner than we anticipated." He paused and drew a thin silver cigarette case from his left breast pocket. Sherb wondered if a smirk moved across the man's face, or if he always looked that way. The young man stuck the cigarette between his lips. "This week, actually."

Sherb ran the man's words through his mind a couple of times, making sure he had heard correctly.

"What part of my property?"

The lieutenant pulled a lighter from his pocket and lit the cigarette, blew smoke upward in a cloud, snapped the lighter shut, unrolled a map. He stuck a finger against the paper, looked around him, turned the map, studied it, glanced around the field again.

"This part through here." His hand made an arc across the largest portion of the Elberta saplings. "We'll be using that for an access road and staging area. And the barn—the contractor needs that for temporary storage."

Balled saplings—more than 200 of them—were against the barn, and Sherb had no intention of putting them anywhere else until they were sold or replanted. Just this morning Bailey Martin had agreed to buy 500 Elbertas, and it would be impossible to get them all balled and moved by the end of the week. He wanted to explain this to the man, tell him why he needed a few more days. How he had to sell the trees to pay for the move, hold the family over until they got settled somewhere. But he knew if he tried, he would only end up shouting.

"Go to the house, boy," he said softly to Levi, who left immediately.

The lieutenant smoked and looked casually over the

Elbertas. He seemed oblivious to Sherb's anger, one that had lain dormant for eight years before budding again last September, when the government appraisers came through from Harriman and told him that once more his family was being forced from their land. The anger had grown all winter, through the months his family was allowed to stay on their own property as a hardship case because Martha had a newborn baby and another one on the way; through the months of trying in vain to find property he could afford, or movers to help him transplant his trees if he did. Sherb hoped he would now have enough self-control to keep his anger from bearing fruit against the arrogant young man in front of him.

Sherb frowned and lowered his head, chewed his upper lip in silence. He reached into the front of his overalls for a twist of tobacco, bit off a chaw and used his tongue to seat it into the familiar pocket of his cheek. When he spoke, someone who did-n't know him might have mistaken his soft tone for kindness.

"As I recall, I've got till March 30th."

"Yes, Mr. McKinney," the young man said indulgently. "But if you read the order you'll see it grants the government the right to take incidental properties before the vacate order takes effect. That's the case here."

"Can't the government wait three more weeks?" The words came out more strident than he intended.

"I'm sorry, but that's impossible."

"Why's it impossible?" He was shouting now. Sherb felt the blood fill his cheeks and throb through his temples; he silently told himself to get control.

"Please, Mr. McKinney, don't make this any more diffi-cult than it has to be." The lieutenant began rolling the map.

Sherb hated the man's condescending tone, the way he spoke past him, over the top of his head.

A black Model-A truck came into sight on the hillside road a few hundred yards away—Jerry Campbell, whose land on the north end of Sherb's property was just outside the big area being taken by the government.

"You'll need to have the barn cleared of belongings by Monday morning. Anything left will be considered abandoned," the young lieutenant said.

"I need that barn. I got thirty bags of fertilizer that'll get ruined if it gets rained on." His voice was almost a cry.

"I'm very sorry, sir. We've tried to accommodate you as much as possible. If you think you have another hardship, you can apply at the district office for consideration."

"You doggone right I got a hardship." Sherb lifted the shovel and swept the blade through the air, indicating the length of his property. "I ain't got nowhere to go, and I can't find no way to move my goods." Sherb resisted the urge to put a hardship on the man's nose—tried to gather up his emotions—told himself the man was just doing his job. But the son of a bitch didn't have to like it.

"You're not the only one, sir. Times are tough all around. But it's for the good of the country." The man was talking down to Sherb, and he knew it. Sherb frowned and rubbed his forehead for a moment. When he finally spoke, his voice was soft and measured.

"And that makes it all right—because I'm doing it for my country?" Sherb looked down to see Levi making his way around the barn toward the house. His voice suddenly rose. "What else do I have to give for my country?"

"I'm sorry, Mr. McKinney," the officer said, and tapped the rolled-up map impatiently against his palm. "That's not my concern."

Sherb's anger rose as many notches as his voice fell.

"Get off my land," he said, almost too softly to be heard.

"I beg your pardon?"

"Get off my property now."

The young man looked off across the Carmans and spoke as if addressing a child. "You're free to behave this way if you wish, Mr. McKinney, but it won't change the facts. It's inevitable."

"I said get off my property now."

The young man continued as if he had not heard.

"The Stone and Webster people will come tomorrow to show you exactly what portions they need. They will bring the papers describing..."

"I'm not going to tell you again." Sherb grabbed the man's upper arm and tried to force him down the hill.

"Get your hands off me, you damned hillbilly," the young officer tried to wrench his arm free, got both hands against Sherb's chest, and shoved hard. Sherb let go the man's arm to break his fall and landed on his back across a row of saplings. The tiny trunks snapped beneath him; the handle of the shovel pressed into his back. The young lieutenant stood over him with a look of horror and disbelief, clenching and unclenching both fists at his sides, the cigarette fallen from his lips. After a moment he wiped his forehead awkwardly, glanced around for his map and cigarette, and forced a smile.

"Well, old timer, it looks like we got off on the wrong..." As quickly as he had fallen, Sherb was up again, the shovel swinging in a quick two-fisted arc. The young man reacted too late, flinching and bringing his hand up in front of his face at the instant the upper corner of the blade slammed with a muted ring into his temple.

The green garrison cap fell from the man's head. He stumbled to his right and brought his left hand the rest of the way to his ear. For the first time he looked Sherb full in the face, his eyes supplicant and vague, his mouth opened for words that did not come. In another second he landed heavily on his side. His body shivered spastically; his arm jerked away from his head, moved up and down, was still. A thin stream of blood and clear liquid trickled from a triangular hole by the ear.

Regret and despair overcame Sherb as quickly as rage a moment before. He stared into the man's still-opened eyes and turned over options in his head: yell for Martha; run to the Campbells' and call Dr. Cox; drag the young man to the truck and take him there himself; ride into Clinton and turn himself in to the sheriff. Instead he knelt, put his ear beside the khaki tie and listened for sounds that did not come.

Sherb began to sob, deep belly sounds of loss and regret—for bottomland, Blackoak Ridge, life. His cries merged with the wail of crows and mockingbirds, dozers, the wind rising again from the southwest.

When he finally raised his head Levi was above him, looking down expressionless at the face of the dead man.

Sherb knew what he had to do.

"Get his legs," he said. Sherb fished in the front pockets for keys and stuffed them into his overalls. He shoved the hat, map and still-burning cigarette into the man's trousers and grabbed the hands, already turning cold.

Neither spoke as they carried the body down the hill and laid it beside the barn. Sherb moved the vehicle—a black staff car—to a spot not visible from the road. At one point Martha stepped out the back door, Verna beside her, Joanne and little Jessie each on a hip. When she saw the body among the balled trees, she shooed Verna inside and followed without a word.

Sherb dug a hole in the empty hog pen, where the ground was soft and wet and bare. The mud got between his fingers and covered his clothes with an animal stink that still lingered two months after the last hog had been sold. He dragged the body to the pit and used the shovel to mound the dirt till there was no sign it had been disturbed.

In the front room Martha, Levi, Lillie and Verna stopped whispering when Sherb came through the door. For a moment all were silent.

"What I done was wrong," Sherb finally began in a half-shout. "I'm sorry. But they's nothing we can do about it now." He looked around the room: Levi and Lillie at the table staring out the window; Verna belly-down on the hearth as if she could read the words of the Watkins catalog in front of her; Martha in the rocker with Joanne in her lap and Jessie on the breast. None met his gaze.

"Don't tell nobody what happened; don't tell nobody

you even seen that Army man. It's a secret. And we got to keep it if you don't want your Daddy going to the electric chair." Halfway out the door he spoke again. "Get your stuff packed. We're leaving before sunup."

"Where we going, Daddy?" Levi looked up at his father for the first time. In the boy's face Sherb saw that what his family was losing had nothing to do with land.

"I don't know, son. We just got to get away from here."

After midnight, Levi followed him in the truck to Lambert's quarry, where they pushed the black staff car from the top into deep water. Sherb stared over the edge until he was sure no one had seen or heard what they had done — until the huge white waves were damped to gentle ripples, and the echo of the splash gave way to the rhythm of crickets and frogs.

MILTON STANLEY grew up the son of Manhattan Project veterans in Oak Ridge. He lives on Blackoak ridge and earns his livelihood doing historical investigations at the old Oak Ridge Gaseous Diffusion Plant.

Don Williams

They Skated to the Limbo All Night Long

See that couple standing-like there, moving without lifting a finger. Now there. They're arcing over that way now, nice little scissor-cut glide and they're against the rail. Coming down at us. Yeah, that's them. That's just about wheat me and Bertie looked like on skates after we both got our growth in. He stood tall and dignified on them just like that, made you wonder how he got around the floor. And he had that square-faced look to him like that man. And he would be gray now like him, if not for the car wreck. He was just that dignified, and when I stood beside him on skates, I was too. Just the merest touch of wheels to the wood and he'd be off halfway across the floor. He was just like that. hard and lean and dignified as a wooden Indian. Dang near dark as one tool. Hold it just a minute, it's time for the change over.

Gentlemen, clear the floor. Ladies only now. All you boys clear the floor!

Well, how far back do you want me to go? I met him in 1961. He was a little feller then, no way to figure he would have growed up like that, and I was just a little bit myself. That's what my daddy called me. Little Bit. I couldn't have been no more than seven and I was in the limbo line. I won it about half the time because I knew how to get up my speed and then squat down and slip under the rod sideways, using my momentum when I turned to keep my inside skate to the wood. I'd lean over until my hair brushed the floor. It was blonde then. Later when we were older, he would talk about how he loved to see my hair do that and he never would admit it but I bet it made him think carnal thoughts. I could see in his eyes he adored me when I did that.

I taught Bertie how to limbo. I really did. He learned to do it and, once he got it down, he dang near defied the laws of God and man getting it done, with his lanky frame.

Before I taught him different, he'd go under the bar, getting low and try to—what's the word for it—*undulate* his back fluid-like, and once in a blue moon he could make it work, but mostly like as not he'd hit that bar with the middle of his back and then go skidding, spraddle-legged across the floor and you couldn't help but laugh. That's how we met. He wiped out once and hit his head and just laid there on the floor, and so I skated over to him where he laid there with his black hair shorn in a burr and he didn't move until I got real low and then he looked up at me and tipped an imaginary hat and grinned like a possum. I helped him to one skate, then stuck my foot behind it and set him back on his bottom for trying to make a fool out of me.

Here, I said, let me show you how that's done, and then I skated to the limbo line and I showed him. What you do is lean hard to the left and sweep your right leg out for balance and bend your neck almost touching the floor on t'other side and cut a sharp turn as you go under so your weight curls you around rather than topples you. That way you'll clear the bar nine times out of ten.

Well, he did it. Took most of a month, coming every Monday on the church night special and every other Saturday night because that's the night his mama and daddy would skate, and it wud'n until the last Saturday of June 1962 that I let him win it because he tried so hard. He was ten by then and I was only nine and he was showing out for me I could tell. His eyes were as big as a girl's and he had them wide in concentration and his big lips pressed together with his determination. Him and Danny Fargo were the last ones out there and they had the stick not eighteen inches off the floor, and Danny came under the bar smirking, pretending he wasn't worried and his skate slipped out and he hit the floor hard. And that last time Bertie come through with the calypso beat playing like it is right now, he liked to have wobbled off center like a top collapsing, but he done it and I was standing at the Coke stand having dropped out the round before to give him a clear shot and he come over and said you could of won it why did you drop out and I give him a look and said because.

He said you want to be with me in the carriage race? And I said maybe and he said come on I'll push and I followed him out there, then scrunched down in the skates in front of him and when he put his hands real low on my waist it took my breath for a minute so that I nearly wiped out on the first turn, but there was four other teams and we whipped 'em all. He knew enough already to get his hands down low on my hips and not to get going too fast and overshoot the mark on the straight-aways as he pushed me, so's we could shift to the inside on the turn and head the others off and that's how we won it.

Couples only now. Boys and girls together. Find you a partner.

But that was a long time ago and I guess we were an item as they say from then on. They started calling us Little Bit and Smidgin cause there wasn't much to him either. See that little runt. That's about how I would imagine he looked long about '64. It took him a while to get his growth in.

When I was twelve, I shot up like Alice in Wonderland and he stayed sort and so he beat me at the limbo skate every week for two years, but it got so he couldn't maneuver me around the rink too good in the carriage race, and do you know it didn't hurt his pride one bit when I suggested we switch positions until his growth come on him good. I pushed him around the arena a time or two and on the third race we won it.

I remember it because that was the first time he ever asked me to skate with him in the couples only skate. Under that crystal ball we slow-dance skated arm in arm side by side and our bodies just fell into the rhythm of it naturally — we were almost exactly the same size then — so that we swayed side by

211

side around the ink like one person, and it was the way it is now with the music soft and the light scattered magic-like, so that rings of light flowed across the walls like reflections off a river in a dream, and we didn't say a word about it that night nor any night for the next year, we just skated slow and easy and dancing-like around the rink. Aye-law.

You know, Bertie wasn't the smartest boy to ever put on a skate, but he was wise, like he was years older than what he was. He would think on things. Sometimes I would see him out there skating alone and he would be thinking on things. I would ask him what it was and he would say he was wondering on who the people were that made the music we skated to. He would try to imagine them in their studio cutting the record and the kind of place they had growed up and who their mamas and daddies were and whether they were saved and things like that. I would just laugh at him and tell him it didn't make any difference as long as they kept making the music and that he thought too much, then I would take his hand and we would skate doubles.

We went to lots of competitions, I would make him go. I would wear my white skirt to match my skates and he would wear his black cowboy shirt and red bandanna I bought him at Penney's, and the night we won the Silver Wheels event, we celebrated by making out in his daddy's Chevy pickup that had the door that wouldn't open from the outside, so he had to leave it cracked when he would get out or else he would have to climb in first on my side which embarrassed him no end.

We took us some Cokes and a bottle of whiskey he had Rodney Shultz to buy for him—first time I ever saw him drink—and I come this close to losing my virginity but I had promised Jesus I would save it. He was my Lord and Master and still is and without Him I don't know what I would have done all these years.

So I wouldn't give in to him because I saw what had become of Becky Clower who had to go off for six months the spring of '65, and Bertie broke up with me for a time when he turned sixteen because I wouldn't go all the way and I said no I was saving myself for when we got married. I hear that virginity is coming back. Do you think that's true? Even some of the boys are declaring their express intent to remain virgins, and I hear there's a thing called Secondary Virginity, where you ca declare yourself made new again, but I don't cotton to that. You can't put it back in the bottle once you've let it out. Anyway, Bertie didn't care anything about me being a virgin. He got his back up, for a while, and quit coming to the rink and so I started dancing with Danny Fargo and we won some trophies but it wudn' nothing to speak of, and then Bertie he come back and busted Danny's nose outside in the parking lot because he saw Danny trying to kiss me. I don't know how long he had been sitting there in his Daddy's pickup. I had seen it over there and so had led Danny in under the light on the corner of the building where I knew Bertie would get a good look at us. He come out of that car walking slow and steady at Danny. There wasn't any doubt what he had in mind and so Danny dropped his arm from around me and went into a boxer's stance, he looked ridiculous with that red cowlick and was moving hands and feet around fancy like and dodging his head back and forth like it was mounted on a spring and Bertie just drew back and cold-cocked him. Danny landed like a sack of flour. Then Bertie led me into the arena and we did the couples-only skate together.

Two weeks later Danny come on the floor and tripped Bertie up big-time during the speed skating. It fractured his ankle and then he waited two months until the cast came off, and he came in and called Danny off the floor and busted his nose again. It's still crooked to this day. Danny tells everybody it got bent during the Gatlinburg game when he tackled Ralph Ogle to preserve the victory on fourth down, but anybody who was here that night knows better. Sometimes Danny still comes by and asks me out and us both middle aged, but I won't go out with him even though I do think Smidgin would smile on it if I was to.

When we was seventeen me and Smidgen took the district crown in the Silver Wheels and then we drove down 411 to Georgia and went by the Justice of the Peace in Dalton and got married at three in the morning. We stayed in a Holiday Inn that night, fanciest place I had stayed up until then and he took me. It was his first time too and not the best night of love we ever had, but it wasn't no time until we was hitting our rhythm. It was the best loving this side of Hollywood. We knew each other's bodies and rhythms and how to make them fit together and I won't ever have another lover.

Ladies clear the floor. Boys only now. Fellas, let's keep it going one way. You there little billygoat. Try to keep it all moving together now. That's it.

Well, he didn't tell me for two weeks more but he had already signed up for the Marines. He come by the night before he shipped out and raced hard, every piddlin' contest, which wudn' as easy as it sounds. There's many a boy that likes nothing better than to show up the hotdogs like we were. Well, he was having none of that. He skated like he had something to prove, like he was chasing something, or something was casing him, or like he just had to get his fill of skating because it would be a long time before he done it again. He drove me hard that night, he did. Drove me to make it the best it ever was and we did. We did. We won the carriage race by a full quarter-lap and I won the girl's side and him the boy's in the speed skating and we placed third in the limbo and us as old as we was. I placed third actually and him fifth, but we didn't make any distinctions about it by then. Whoever placed best, why hit was for both of us. And when it come time for Couples Only, Joe Merton, who owned the place then, dimmed the lights and everybody stood out of respect and we danced the last one alone to "Soldier Boy" and Joe announced over the speaker, "Let's hear it for our own soldier boy, Bert McGee. He's not a Smidgin anymore."

And I reckon he wasn't. He was tall and dignified. He

didn't smile as we went around the rink. He just pressed his lips together and looked in every boy and girl's face and he waved at everybody there. And boys held out their hands over the railing and he touched them with his fingers as he went by and when he stopped, Danny come up and shook his hand and my girlfriends cried and hugged Smidgin and then each other, and even grownups were sniffing because Smidgin wouldn't be here with us come the Monday Church Night Special.

He came home several times over the next two years, but it wasn't the same. He never did race anymore. He would just come in and skate.

I was working the concession stand by then and already socking away my savings. Bertie would come in and just skate for hours round the rink. You see how undignified so many people look on wheels? I mean just look out there. Goosenecked and arms flapping and feet kicking up.

Well, Bertie never was like that, least of all after he come back from Vietnam. It was all different by then. It seemed like overnight the place changed. Joe had installed colored lights and the new high-fidelity sound system and it drew a new crowd. And all the girls wore these swishy little skirts and all the boys had their hair long. You could smell marijuana on some occasions.

Bertie would come here first thing, still wearing his uniform, and his face would look pained like he didn't understand something. Then his face would change to an expression of acceptance and he would go to skating. He looked like a statue on wheels the way he would go around the rink with his face blank and his strong arms at his side. He would lean this way and that and, with just the barest of nudges of his feet, he would ride round and around for hours just thinking on things. I would get out there with him on the slow-dance songs and we was one then. Kick, follow-through, glide, kick, follow-through, glide, Then I would go back and he would do it all alone again. Stolid, I think the word is. Maybe just stolid. Whichever it is, that was him.

After the place would shut down some nights he would still be going round and around, but he never competed airy a time atter that.

We bought the rink in 1971 and he took over the books while schooling on the GI Bill. He changed the music back to the Four Seasons and Elvis and Ricky Nelson, and took out the colored lights. The disco craze about did us in because he wouldn't give in to the coke heads and turn us into a rink like you might imagine out of Saturday Night Fever, but we squeaked through some ways.

There was nothing about the night he got in the wreck that would give anybody a clue. He come up where I was working the booth like I am now, spinning records and making change and he asked for two twenties, said he was going to get some small bills to set up for Saturday night. He said, "See ya later, Little Bit," and I said, "Bye, Smidgin," and he said kind of up-beat, "Save the slow-dance for me," and it wasn't ten minutes later that the phone rung and it was the police saying that he had been in a accident. He had give up the ghost by the time I reached the hospital. I identified the body. There wasn't a scratch on him that you could see. I set in there for the longest time while different ones come by the hospital Danny and Benny and Joe and my girlfriends and lots of the regulars from the rink. Mama tried to get me to leave but I wouldn't you see we was one we had always been one and I wanted to lay down there with him and die too but i didn't. I've studied on it a lot of times and read my Bible trying to figure it out but it don't square no way you look at it. They's nothing in it for Jesus to take him. He was just a good man and now the world's shy one good man, but Jesus is still my Lord and Master.

I went out to where whoever it was that sideswiped him and made him hit that pole, but they never did catch them and the wreck was already cleared away. I would've druther seen his blood on the road just to get it all set in my mind, how this caused his death, but except for a little smear of blue paint and a few scars on the pole there was nothing much to see. It didn't even bust his windshield. I did go by Eddies' Garage the next day and look at the Mustang. I didn't look that bad, but Eddie asked me if I wanted to total it out, he'd take care of it, so I did. I got the life insurance money too and paid off the mortgage on the rink and it was six months before his goneness really sunk in. You look up and expect to see him standing in the doorway to the record booth or over at the concession stand booths working the books or out there skating, and finally when you don't for about the hundredth time it sinks in that he is gone.

I took his lead and spent many a night skating round and around no end to it. I thought of selling the place off and taking up real estate or something that wouldn't hold his memory, but I couldn't bring myself to do hit. So I come here and work the booth and spin records and make change. Every few years people still take to Elvis and the Four Seasons and the young Beatles, and so we experience an upswing in the business.

When I see somebody like Linda and Ronnie Delozier over there, tall and square-shouldered gliding around with their arms around one another, I imagine it's him and me. Smidgin would be gray like Ronnie by now and I bet sill in shape like him. And sometimes when I see some piss-ant kids doing the hokey-pokey I think how we done it. There's nights I turn the crystal ball on and just sit here with lights sprinkling the walls and no music playing and I feel him in here inhabiting the place.

All right. Everybody now. Let's skate. Come on. Get on the floor. This 'un's for everybody. Last chance. It's closing time.

Oh, one more thing. The night he was killed, I left in a hurry as you might imagine. The arm that rejects them old-timey records was lifted up off the record player and I had pulled the door to the booth closed behind me, and those who was there that night said the limbo kept playing over and over. Even after the limbo winner was made clear, the record played on so that everybody was standing there on the side and the floor was empty, and they all just stood there until the song played through, and then Linda Sue got out there on the floor and then another one and another, and the music played all by itself and nobody was there to turn it off and then they all go out on the floor and they was some of them skated to the limbo all night long. It's still talked about.

DON WILLIAMS is the founding editor of *New Millenium Writings*, and he is also a columnist and former feature editor for the *Knoxville News-Sentinel*. His work also appears in the Tennessee bicentennial anthology, *HomeWorks*. Williams lives in Sevier County with his wife and three children.

Marcia E. Williams

Hawk Month

Tradition may mark November as the time of elections, Thanksgiving, post-Halloween, pre-Christmas festivities. But we think of it as hawk month. This goes back to the first year we lived in Franklin, TN.

We'd been in our home, just half a mile from the Confederate monument in the town square, since the beginning of July. On a bitter November morning, a crash interrupts our preparation for work. Not the tire-screeching, horn-blowing, pause-while-you-wait to hear if there is impact of metal-on-metal kind. Worse. More like the time I accidentally dropped a glass bottle on the terrazzo floor of my parents' Florida home. Multiplied a hundred times.

"David!" I scream as my husband simultaneously calls my name.

"What was that?" we both ask.

"I bet the chandelier in the dining room fell," he says. We scurry downstairs expecting to find that it has crashed down like the final scene of the movie, "War of the Roses." Entering the dining room, we see that the chandelier is still hanging, but then we freeze: one end to the other is covered with shards of glass. A wall of cold air hits us and draws our eyes to the former location of a 3' by 4' window.

Do other people have these problems? Do their windows spontaneously explode at 6:30 a.m. in November? Other people have other problems. Their windows don't explode. As it turns out, neither has ours. Our surprise is dwarfed by that of the hawk staring at us from across the room.

Well over a foot tall, this is one big bird. Baffled too. This is not what he's planned for his morning, either. David and I breathe a collective sigh of relief, although, upon reflection, relief seems a strange emotion upon finding a wild, live, meat-eating, bird with a five-foot wing span, standing in the middle of smithereens of glass in your dining room while you're trying to get ready for work. We're glad he blasted in while we were there. Consider the alternative of returning from work to a darkened house to shiver in the November air, find the broken window, fear for burglars, and call the police from a neighbors' phone, only to find a hawk.

We've already found this hawk and work will wait. First we videotape him (any non-believers, give me a call). Then we identify him: Cooper's hawk. According to our *Golden Guide to Birds*, he eats wild birds, poultry, mammals, vertebrates, and insects. We shoo our terriers out of the dining room and feed the hawk some barbecue.

He moves to the fanlight above the back door. David finesses him onto a broom handle and eases him out. He bumps the storm door and flies back in to his roost, big wings flapping images of Hitchcock's "The Birds" into our minds. The second time, David succeeds in easing him down from the fanlight, across the door frame, and outside the house. The hawk, although still dazed, flies off.

The glass people who repaired the window point out the last one they'd fixed—upstairs sewing room. It's proved popular. Another hawk takes it out again two Novembers later. Three years ago again in November, a third hawk takes out a side window in the sewing room.

Just before Thanksgiving, I was shortening a pair of pants and heard a bump at the window. I threw myself on the floor, screamed, and covered my head with my arms expecting the window to explode upon hawk impact. False alarm. This time. But in November, in downtown Franklin, one cannot be too cautious.

::

MARCIA WILLIAMS lives and writes in Franklin, and had a story appear last year in *Our Voices*, an anthology of Williamson County writers.

Wanda A. Wright

The Stargazer and the Dare-Devil

*Best wishes
to a fellow writer
Wanda Wright*

It was with unbridled excitement that Claudia and I unfastened the rickety gate as soon as the car was parked, and rode it as far as it would go. Claudia usually leaped off the gate before it stopped, leaving me to ride alone until it dragged to a halt, and then bounded down the path yelling, "Hurry up, slowpoke." She was headed to the crest of the hill where we would stand side by side and gaze at the top of the barn roof.

Jumping off a low-slung, tin barn roof into Daddy's arms was the first thing we did each time we went to my granddaddy's farm, so I purposely lagged behind, stuffing my pockets with sycamore balls to throw in the creek later in the day. Mother and Daddy and I stopped long enough to deposit our quilts and picnic cooler and to admire my granddaddy's Farmall tractor resting alone in a field after a hard week's work before catching up with Claudia, dancing impatiently on the hill. The flour of us stood together suspended in time, surveying the plum thicket and apple orchard that guarded the barn below. My only thoughts were of the impending jump from the roof.

Then off Claudia and I sprinted down the hill to the barn, our bare feet making slapping noises on the dried, grassy path. We stood bouncing and giggling and wringing our hands in anticipation until Mother and Daddy got to the barn. Daddy immediately lifted Claudia onto the roof while I waited below, wrestling with the butterflies in my stomach. Before I was ready I felt Daddy's strong hands under my armpits and felt the adrenal rush push away the butterflies as my feet left the ground and I flew through the air up over his head landing on the edge of the roof. Daddy never took his hands away until he

221

knew we were steady on the roof and he laughingly asked the same question before backing away, "Who jumping first?" Without hesitation, Claudia dove into his waiting arms. As soon as her feet hit the ground she began pestering me to "jump, jump!" No matter how many times I had performed this ritual, I still had to be coaxed, and only after threats of leaving me on the roof and when my bare feet began burning on the hot tin would I make my valiant leap. Why did it take me so long to jump? Perhaps the reason for my reluctance was the enchantment and the solitary freedom I felt as I stood on the roof alone, watching the birds soaring and circling the cornfield, calling to one another in flight. Maybe I was held captive by the old majestic, magical chimney that harbored special secrets waiting to be discovered. It stood stalwartly and bravely alone in the distance, beckoning, counting on our visit.

The trip to Pappy's farm in those days was unvarying. It was the daredevil versus the dawdler wherever we went. Claudia was the first to shinny up the apple tree to pick apples for the cider press, calling below for me to "come on up." I waited underneath for Daddy to shake the tree so Mother and I could pick them up off the ground before I ventured to the top. What was it that kept me out of the vibrating apple tree with Claudia? I remember watching the leaves quivering and liking the sound of their rustling and swishing as Daddy shook the tree limb furiously. I remember the plunking noise the apples made when they hit the ground and the buzzing sound the yellowjackets made swarming around the rotten apples lying under the tree. I liked watching the shower of apples as they fell from the tree and rolled every which way, bumping into each other.

And who trekked into the barn with Daddy, swatting down spider webs as she went, to get the cider press? Claudia. I much preferred standing in the doorway, letting the cool air burst out of hiding onto my face and inhaling the muskiness that seeped out into the hot sun from the dark room. As Daddy opened the barn door, I was intrigued by the patterns of sunlight filtering through the cracks and the cider press, standing idly alone in the corner marking time. Together, Daddy and Claudia dragged the cider press out of the bar, and Claudia began tossing apples into its hungry mouth. I positioned myself in the stream of dust particles dancing in rays of sunshine, picturing myself as a fairy traipsing along the imaginary trail of dust.

Likewise, when we hiked over to Daddy's old homeplace where the rock chimney and a half-set of stairs had been left standing by the ravages of time, it was Claudia who went hopping down the pathway, leaping over black racers unafraid and carelessly slapping away bees and flies. While she leaped over the snakes, I was mesmerized by the marks its slithering body was leaving in the dust. I was content wandering serenely along the tangled path overgrown from years of neglect, dodging cow patties and watching strange bugs rolling little black balls down a nowhere path. As Claudia bounded up the crumbling steps of the old house, despite Mother's pleas, I stepped gingerly over what was left of the house's foundation, eyeing carefully the old pieces of broken pottery and discarded toys lying forlornly in the dirt—they would give me clues about the young boy that had become my dad. Before we left, I would have unearthed a small relic from the past to take home and analyze.

Our wide swing around the farm brought us back all too soon to the blackberry thicket, our last and most dreaded stop before the picnic and the drive home. Mother had taught us to be cautious of snakes and not to eat the blackberries without being washed, but she had no control over the chiggers we would take home hidden deep within the crevices of our clothing and our bodies. Perspiration rolled down our faces, our clothes clung to us like flypaper, and we slapped miserably at sweat bees as we filled our buckets with the dark, plump blackberries that promised cobbler for several Sundays. Claudia ate as many blackberries as she picked and when Mother wasn't looking, I popped an occasional unwashed berry in my mouth as a reward for enduring the torture of the heat and the thorns. As soon as Mother said enough berries, we headed out of the thicket to the spring as fast as we could. In our eagerness for water from the spring, Claudia and I both ran carelessly among the briars, snagging our clothes and scratching our tender skin. But a hundred scratches on our arms and legs was worth one drink of water from the spring.

The best part of the spring was the coolness that enveloped me as I walked down the steps alone, after Daddy and Claudia finished dipping out icy cold water for us to drink. I descended the steps and let the chill penetrate my clothing and my thoughts. I ran my hands gently over the soft, cushiony moss that covered the walls, and I inhaled the heady, earthy smell. Then I squatted down and immersed my scratched arms into the soothing water where water striders skimmed back and forth gracefully along the surface. White puffy clouds drifted across the blue sky as I sat crouched on the last step, staring at their reflection and memorizing the chipped rim around the mouth of the white enamel dipper, and breathing in remembrances of the smell of mint growing along the water's edge. I loved everything about the spring—the dipper balanced precariously on a ledge opposite the steps, the spongy green moss, and the water striders darting among the mint.

Daydreams don't last long, and mine were splintered by the picnic call from Claudia. I hurried up from the dampness of the spring back into the sultry reality of the day. I ran to the quilt and flopped down, exhausted and invigorated. After satisfying my ravenous appetite with bologna and crackers and dressed eggs from the picnic basket, I lay on my back and watched the clouds play hide and seek with the leaves of the ancient sycamore. I could feel the contradictory warm and cool as the leaves parted and came back together. Such tranquility. The day was perfect—despite Claudia's battle with caterpillars that dropped from the sycamore into her shirt, and despite her determination in dragging the quilt this way and that to find just the right spot. Even her squirminess failed to spoil our lighthearted, peaceful mood.

Those perfect days, however, no longer exist because the farm has long since been sold, the homeplace and barn have been razed, the apple tree and blackberry thickets are gone, and the two sisters have grown up. Through the years our distinct personalties have remained intact, but they have also become the same—entwined and inseparable. Claudia persists in rushing through life headlong, much like she did when she was younger, but age and the passing of time have allowed her to slow down, and together we enjoy the slanting rays of the evening sun on an old barn and marvel at a sunset's shimmer on the water. I am still serene and reflective, pondering memories from my past, and I continue to internalize the miracles of the smell of rain beating down the dust on a hot summer day, or the drops of dew on a lacy spider web in early morning. But I, too, realize time is short. So frequently, I break away from my stargazing and dawdling, and Claudia and I wind our way down tangled paths, leaping over snakes daredevil style.

WANDA A. WRIGHT lives in Franklin and has taught school in near-by Spring Hill for the past twenty-five years. Her work also appears in *Dream Days*, an anthology of the Southeast Writers Association.